IELTS Academic Writing 8+

How to write high-scoring 8+ answers for the IELTS exam. Packed full of examples, practice questions and top tips.

www.How2Become.com

Orders: Please contact How2Become Ltd, Suite 3, 40 Churchill Square Business Centre, Kings Hill, Kent ME19 4YU.

You can order through Amazon.co.uk under ISBN 9781912370375, via the website www.How2Become.com, Gardners or Bertrams.

ISBN: 9781912370375

First published in 2018 by How2Become Ltd.

Copyright © 2018 How2Become.

All rights reserved. Apart from any permitted use under UK copyright law, no part of this publication may be reproduced or transmitted in any form or by any means, electronic or mechanical, including photocopying, recording, or any information, storage or retrieval system, without permission in writing from the publisher or under licence from the Copyright Licensing Agency Limited. Further details of such licenses (for reprographic reproduction) may be obtained from the Copyright Licensing Agency Ltd, Saffron House, 6-10 Kirby Street, London EC1N 8TS.

Typeset for How2Become Ltd by Gemma Butler.

Disclaimer

Every effort has been made to ensure that the information contained within this guide is accurate at the time of publication. How2Become Ltd is not responsible for anyone failing any part of any selection process as a result of the information contained within this guide. How2Become Ltd and their authors cannot accept any responsibility for any errors or omissions within this guide, however caused. No responsibility for loss or damage occasioned by any person acting, or refraining from action, as a result of the material in this publication can be accepted by How2Become Ltd.

The information within this guide does not represent the views of any third-party service or organisation.

As part of this product you have also received FREE access to online tests that will help you to pass your IELTS tests.

To gain access, simply go to:

www.PsychometricTestsOnline.co.uk

Get more products for passing any test at:

www.How2Become.com

Hello and welcome to your guide: *IELTS Academic Writing 8+*. In this guide, we will give you a comprehensive breakdown of how to score an 8+ in the IELTS writing section (academic test mode). Using sample questions, strategies and tips, by the end of this guide you will be in a fantastic position to score highly in your assessment.

So, without further ado, let's begin!

What is IELTS?

IELTS stands for International English Language Testing System. It is essentially a system which measures the language and writing proficiency of people who want to work or study in a country where English is the primary language. The scoring is done on a scale of 9, with 9 being the highest (at expert level) and 1 being the lowest (at non-user level). This book is designed to help you score an 8+ in your IELTS assessment.

There are two versions of the IELTS, which are as follows:

Academic. IELTS Academic is designed for candidates applying to higher education or professional registration.

General Training. IELTS General Training is designed for candidates migrating to the UK, Canada or Australia, or who are applying for secondary education or work experience/training in an environment where English is the primary language.

Both versions of the IELTS will assess your listening, reading, writing and speaking skills. The listening and speaking elements are the same for both tests, but the reading and writing elements will differ.

In this guide, we will be focusing purely on the **IELTS Academic Writing** assessment.

IELTS Academic

Before we begin focusing on the actual writing part of the assessment, it's important to break down the other areas of the test. After all, you'll need to prepare for every single element if you want to pass. There are four elements to the IELTS Academic, which are as follows:

Listening. The listening exercise lasts for 30 minutes in total. You will listen to a total of four recordings of native English speakers, and will then need to answer questions based on what you've heard.

The recordings will be as follows:

- A conversation set in a regular, social context. For example, you might listen to two people speaking about the weather (particularly common in Britain!)
- A monologue (one person speaking) again in a regular, social context. For example, you might listen to someone speaking about their trip to the shops.
- A conversation between a number of people (a maximum of 4) set in an educational or work-based context. For example, you might hear a teacher talking with their student about a piece of work that they've given in.
- A monologue (one person speaking) on a specific academic topic. For example, you might hear an extract of a teacher giving a lecture.

When assessing the listening test, you will be scored against the following categories:

- How well you understand the main ideas in the recording.
- How much detail you have picked up on from the recording.
- The opinions and beliefs of the speakers in the recording.
- The purpose of specific wording. For example, if someone in the recording says 'Stop!' then you might be asked to explain what they are referring to.
- Your ability to follow the development and train of conversation.

Speaking. The speaking exercise lasts for 11-14 minutes. You will be tested against your use of spoken English, with the test being recorded for marking purposes. You'll need to answer all of the questions/tasks verbally. There are three parts to this test:

- In part 1, you'll need to answer spoken questions in relation to subjects such as your family, your home life, your work, your general interests and your studies. This part of the test should last for approximately 5 minutes.
- In part 2, you will need to speak about a particular topic for two minutes in total. You'll be given a card which gives you the topic, and then will have one minute to prepare before the exercise starts.

Following your spoken monologue, the examiner will ask you a couple of questions based on what you've said.

- In part 3, you will be asked some extra questions about the topic from part 2. These questions will be more in-depth and will explore further issues related to the topic. This part of the test will last for approximately 5 minutes.

As we've mentioned, the listening and speaking elements are the same, regardless of if you are taking IELTS Academic or IELTS General Training. However, the reading and writing are different. Here's what the reading entails, for IELTS Academic:

IELTS Academic: Reading

The IELTS Academic reading exercise will last for 1 hour in total. There will be 40 questions, all designed to assess your reading skill/level. Amongst the things being marked are:

- How well you can understand the main ideas in a text.
- How efficiently you can 'skim read'.
- How well you can understand logic and arguments for/against from the text.
- How well you can identify and recognise writers' opinions, and the purpose for which they are writing.
- How much detail you can remember, having read a text.

The test itself will encompass three long texts. The texts will vary. So, you might get one text which is particularly descriptive, one text which is factually based and one text which is analytical. All of the texts will be taken from either a book, a journal, a magazine or a newspaper. The texts have been deliberately chosen to be appropriate for people applying for a university course or wanting professional registration.

Now, let's move onto the main subject of our book: the writing task!

IELTS Academic: Writing Format

The IELTS Academic writing assessment is a comprehensive test of your writing skills. Just like the reading assessment, the exercises have been deliberately chosen to be appropriate for people applying for a university course or wanting professional registration.

The test will last for 60 minutes, and will assess elements such as:

- Your ability to write clearly and concisely.
- Your ability to accurately summarise data.
- Your ability to describe.
- Your ability to explain.
- Your ability to identify arguments, and respond to them.
- Your ability to write formally.
- Your ability to use language to persuade and inform.
- Your grasp of grammar, spelling and punctuation.

There are a total of two tasks in the IELTS Academic writing assessment. The second task is the most important in terms of your writing band score, contributing to double that of task 1.

The tasks are as follows:

Task 1

In this task, you will be given a graph, table or chart. Your job is to look at the image and then summarise or explain the information that's being presented. You might also be given a diagram of a machine, or a device, and then asked to explain how it functions and how it works. The main aim of the assessment is to see how well you can identify important information and trends/patterns, whilst giving an overview of said information in an accurate and academic/formal style. Your main priority should be to include the most important/relevant aspects of the image in front of you. You should try to include minor details if you can, but you will score higher if you focus on the more important elements of the image.

You will be given 20 minutes to complete this task. The aim should be to write 150 words in total. If you write any less than this then you will be penalised. You will not lose marks for exceeding the word count, but you should not spend any longer than 20 minutes on this task. You will also be penalised if you go off topic at any point during your written response, or you fail to adhere to basic requirements, such as sentence structure, grammar, spelling and punctuation. You must write in full and clear sentences, do not use bullet points or short-hand text.

When taking the test, you'll be provided with an answer booklet in which to write your responses.

Task 2

In this task, you will be given a topic and then asked to write about it in an academic/formal style. The topic will be given to you in the form of a prompt. For example, you might be given a statement which reads, 'Zoos are immoral and should be banned.' You'll then need to respond to this statement, either arguing for or against, with detailed analysis on why you believe what you believe. You should try to support your answer with evidence, and you are allowed to use examples based on your own personal experience. You must make sure that you focus on the statement in the question. For example, if the statement reads, 'Zoos are immoral, they should be banned,' then you need to focus your answer on zoos, not just on lions, or whatever your favourite animal is. While you could use the plight of some animals kept within zoos to strengthen your argument, this should not be the main focus of your argument.

The minimum word count for this exercise is 250 words, and you will have 40 minutes to complete the assessment. Again, falling under the word count will result in you being penalised. The marks for task 2 are twice that of task 1, meaning that failure to complete this exercise will greatly harm your chances of scoring highly.

During this assessment, the main elements that are being tested are in relation to the fluency of your writing and vocabulary. You are also being tested on how well your response is structured, how well it uses persuasive language, and how well it cites information and ideas. Basically, you need to put together a coherent and logical response, paying attention to grammar, spelling and punctuation, whilst addressing the main statement from the question.

Now that we've explained about the different elements of the test, let's move onto the really important stuff – how to pass!

General Writing Tips

In English, punctuation consists of a number of symbols, marks, or signs which are deployed around letters and words, in order to convey the writer's intended meaning. The use of spacing also comes under punctuation. All the different punctuation marks perform different jobs within a sentence, all of which are important.

Punctuation is a good place to start when discussing writing, as it allows us to give meaning and form to our words and sentences. Without punctuation, comprehending writing of any length would be nigh on impossible. This is the point of punctuation – to aid understanding.

Another reason to begin by looking at punctuation is because its rules are mostly set in stone. For academic writing, personal style should not affect how you use punctuation – at least not too much. Each punctuation mark has its own specific use, which helps to convey a specific meaning within a sentence.

So, using different punctuation marks in different places within the same sentence will alter its meaning.

For example:

- *A woman, without her man, is nothing.*
- *A woman: without her, man is nothing.*

The full stop (.)

Of course, the main use of a full stop is to show where a sentence ends. The examples below are all 'complete' sentences, which are what you should be writing in.

For example:

- *American writer Mark Twain was born in Missouri.*
- *The tallest mountain in Ecuador is called 'Chimborazo'.*
- *The sale of vehicles represents the United Kingdom's second largest export.*

While this is simple, let's look now at what constitutes a complete sentence.

A complete sentence will always contain at least one main clause. A main clause will contain a subject as well as a verb to act on this subject.

Have another look at the example sentences used above. This time, you will find the subjects of the sentences highlighted, and the verbs of the sentences underlined.

- *American writer Mark Twain was born in Missouri.*
- *The tallest mountain in Ecuador is called 'Chimborazo'.*
- *The sale of vehicles represents the United Kingdom's second-largest export.*

If you are unsure as to whether a sentence you have written is incomplete, try to identify its subject(s) and verb(s). If you can't, you may not have written a complete sentence – you may have written a sentence fragment.

Examples of Sentence Fragments

- *Riding on the coattails of another's successes.*
- *To visit her friend on St. Patrick's Day.*
- *And went to Dudley for work experience.*

As you can see, the above 'sentences' do not show verbs acting on subjects – their subjects are implied. In the first one, we do not know *who* has been riding on the coattails. Therefore, the phrase is merely a sentence fragment. As a general rule, you should avoid using sentence fragments in your writing.

The comma (,)

The comma is a deceptively difficult piece of punctuation to use. For this reason, it is often misused and/or overused. The difficulty lies in the fact that there are many different writing situations that require the use of a comma, and many situations where its use would be incorrect.

So, we can say that there are many different types of comma.

The simplest use of the comma is to separate nouns in a list.

For example:

- *The government is prioritising education, health, and libraries.*
- *The new signing brings pace, power, and vision to the squad.*
- *Bleak House, Great Expectations, and Little Dorrit are all works by Charles Dickens.*

Note: The examples given above all employ the 'Oxford Comma' or 'serial comma' (a comma between the penultimate item in the list and 'and'), which is generally seen as being optional.

The Oxford Comma

Those in favour of the Oxford comma suggest it can bring clarity to certain situations. For example, consider the following two versions of this sentence:

- *'I love my children, Dracula, and Frankenstein.'*
- *'I love my children, Dracula and Frankenstein.'*

As you can see, the use of the Oxford comma in the first sentence makes it crystal clear that the writer loves their children, as well as the two characters of Dracula and Frankenstein. The other version of the sentence could suggest something rather different – that the writer's children *are* Dracula and Frankenstein.

As when listing nouns, commas are also used to separate listed adjectives and adverbs. Think about when you want to describe something with more than one word in a row. You'd use commas to separate these words!

For example:

- *The great, grey mountain peak stood ominously above the village.*
- *Move the rod slowly, precisely, and decisively if you want to catch a fish.*
- *The lavender plant is known for its fragrant, colourful, and attractive flowers.*

Another extremely common use of the comma is to separate clauses within sentences.

For example:

- *Ricardo bought a new pair of shoes, but did not get his watch repaired as intended.*
- *As the room filled with water, the family became more and more afraid.*
- *I've never watched musicals, and don't intend to start doing so now.*

While this type of comma might end up being the most commonly appearing one in your writing, make sure you use it correctly. In other words, beware the comma splice.

The Comma Splice

A comma splice occurs when a writer employs a comma to link two independent clauses – clauses that could make sense on their own as sentences. As shown above, a comma can be used to separate such clauses within one sentence, but with the use of other connective words like 'and' or 'but'. So, when a comma is used to separate two independent clauses (clauses that could make sense on their own as sentences), an error occurs.

For example (these are INCORRECT sample sentences):

- *A lioness's top speed is around 50mph, they can run fast in short bursts.*
- *I enjoy playing the piano, I use it to relax.*
- *The Battle of Maidstone took place in June 1648, it ended in victory for the parliamentarians.*

The problem with these sentences is that a comma is not sufficient to link them. The two clauses either need to be in their own sentences, or connectives/a different punctuation mark needs to be used. See below for correct versions of the three wrong examples given above. The highlighted areas show what has been changed to make the sentences correct.

- *A lioness's top speed is around 50mph; they can run fast in short bursts.*
- *I enjoy playing the piano. I use it to relax.*
- *The Battle of Maidstone took place in June 1648, and it ended in victory for the parliamentarians.*

Similarly, commas are also used to separate introductory parts of a sentence from its main clause.

For example:

- *After arriving home from the festival, Nathan fired up his computer.*
- *Despite initial disagreement, the deal was struck relatively quickly.*
- *Fortunately, there was not too much damage.*

A further use of the comma is to separate 'extra' details of a sentence from its main clause. In these cases, two commas would be used to contain the 'extra' information from the main content of the sentence. A good way to check if you are using this type of comma correctly is to take out the 'extra' information and see if the main clause makes sense by itself. If it does, you're looking good.

For example:

- *The beach, which was empty and serene, was her favourite place to spend time.*
- *Seoul's Olympic Park, which played host to the 1988 Olympics, was renovated in 2011.*
- *Rahul, my cousin, graduated from university this summer.*

Commas also have an important role to play when writing dialogue or direct speech. Namely, they are used to separate the direct speech from the rest of the sentence.

For example:

- *"It certainly is striking," he said, "but it's not my cup of tea."*
- *"I'm warning you," she whispered, "behave yourself or you're out of here."*
- *"As you can see," said the tour guide, "the area becomes quite different following a rainstorm."*

> Note: The rules surrounding comma splices and direct speech are murky at best. In many situations, such as when writing novels, a comma splice as we've discussed is often not seen as a mistake – more of a stylistic choice. (See the second example above.) In academic writing, should it be relevant, it's probably best to err on the side of caution. Perhaps ask a teacher, tutor, or advisor about their preference on the matter!

The colon (:)

While the comma is deceptively difficult to use, the colon is deceptively easy. That is to say, its uses are relatively few and clear.

Firstly, its most simple use is to introduce listed nouns.

For example:

- *The ingredients are simple: milk, eggs, flour, and butter.*
- *There were myriad treasures underneath: precious stones, jewellery, coins, everything.*
- *She wrote down what was most important to her: her dog, her friends, and work.*

> Note: When using colons in this way, you should make sure that the introductory part of the sentence would make sense on its own. For example, you should NOT write – 'The ingredients are: milk, eggs, flower, and butter.' You would not need to use a colon in this case. So, the colon is not <u>required</u> for every situation to do with introducing lists, although it can add clarity and style.

Another prominent use of the colon is to reveal and develop themes and ideas within a sentence. While this sounds complicated, you'll see from the examples that it's actually quite simple.

For example:

- *There was one thing on his mind: vengeance.*
- *The coach was under no illusions: if he lost one more game, his career was over.*
- *The world is embroiled in an ongoing crisis: stagnating wages and soaring prices.*

This is most often done for emphasis.

Again, the part of the sentence that falls before the colon should make sense on its own. However, in creative writing, you may wish to flout this rule should it muscle in on your style too much.

The semicolon (;)

The semicolon is probably the most complained-about punctuation mark. Be it confused novices struggling to get to grips with it, or smug veterans maligning its misuse, you'll have heard people arguing about the semicolon.

In truth, it's not that interesting, or even that difficult to use.

Its main use is to separate two independent clauses that are closely related. This means that the two halves of the sentence must be able to make sense by themselves. In other words, your sentence containing the semicolon could feasibly be split into two perfect sentences.

However, the choice not to split them in this way, and instead employ a semicolon, would be a choice to emphasise a link of some sort between the two clauses.

For example:

- *Graham was easily frightened; the slightest noise could startle him.*
- *Audrey had a very specific taste in film; she would watch old comedies but nothing else.*
- *I'm karate mad; I train every day for at least 3 hours.*

Think back to the section about the comma splice – the semicolon could stand in for an erroneous comma in these situations.

Also, make sure that you are not using a semicolon where a colon would be more appropriate. In many situations, if what follows your semicolon could not make sense as its own sentence, a colon would be more appropriate.

However, in cases like this, it may be preferable to rewrite your sentence into two sentences, or use a comma and a connective!

For example:

INCORRECT:	In 1982, Mexico suffered a terrible tragedy; the eruption of El Chichón.
CORRECT:	In 1982, Mexico suffered a terrible tragedy: the eruption of El Chichón.
CORRECT:	In 1982, Mexico suffered a terrible tragedy. It was the eruption of El Chichón.

Note: See how 'It was' was added to the second part of the third example to create a second complete sentence.

General Writing Tips **21**

Another use of the semicolon is to separate items in a list which are long or convoluted in some way. This is done to provide clarity and understanding where simply using commas would not have been sufficient.

For example:

- *Belligerents of the War of the Roses included: Henry VI, House of Lancaster; Henry VII, House of Tudor; Margaret of Anjou, House of Valois-Anjou; and Edward IV, House of York.*

As you can see, using semicolons to separate the listed items here allows the use of the comma within the listed items themselves, and makes it clear the Houses belong with the respective rulers. It even has the use of an Oxford semicolon…

So, let's look at what this list would have looked like without the use of the semicolon:

For example (this is an INCORRECT sample sentence):

- *Belligerents of the War of the Roses included: Henry VI, House of Lancaster, Henry VII, House of Tudor, Margaret of Anjou, House of Valois-Anjou, and Edward IV, House of York.*

This sentence is much more confusing; the reader has been led to believe that the Houses are separate from the rulers. The semicolon is the saviour of this situation.

The hyphen (-)

The hyphen (-) is another potentially tricky piece of punctuation to use correctly. It is often confused with the dash (–), its longer cousin. We'll cover the dash in the next section.

Despite potential hurdles, the hyphen has a clear set of rules surrounding its use. However, it can get complicated. Let's look at a few examples.

Hyphens are most often used within adjectives that are made up of two (or more) words and other compound words.

For example:

- *Twenty-first century literature.*

- *An off-the-cuff remark.*
- *A self-diagnosed illness.*

However, it is easy to make mistakes and use hyphens when there is no need to. For example, if you wanted to use 'off the cuff' adverbially rather than as an adjective (describing a verb rather than a noun), then you should not use hyphens.

For example:

- *The remark was made off the cuff.*

Also, hyphens should not be employed in sentences where these types of adjectives follow the noun. In the first three examples above, they precede the noun.

For example:

- *The remark was off the cuff.*
- *The century was the twenty first.*
- *The illness was self-diagnosed.*   (*This is an exception! See below.*)

However, in a quirk of the language, the same is not true of compound words containing the word 'self', such as 'self-diagnosed'. When using this word following a noun, the hyphen stays.

For example:

- *The illness was self-diagnosed.*
- *They considered themselves to be quite self-sufficient.*
- *The archetypal villain is ruthless and self-serving.*

The dash (–)

The dash, often confused with the hyphen, is a completely different punctuation mark to its shorter counterpart. It serves an entirely different purpose within a sentence, and is in no way interchangeable!

The main use of the dash is to signal an 'interruption' within a sentence. This could be in the shape of a change of subject, theme, or tone. When writing dialogue, even, this could be a literal interruption!

However, in academic writing, the use of the dash would be a stylistic choice to represent a change of direction within a sentence, or to provide juxtaposition between two clauses in a sentence. Overall though, it's probably good advice to use the dash sparingly. See below for some examples of its use.

For example:

- *Edgar was set to become Earl of Gloucester and inherit his father's title – but Edmund had other ideas.*
- *Rules are rules, of course – yet they are made to be broken.*
- *She was shy, quiet, and unassuming – or so she'd have you believe.*

Another way the dash is used is similar to how commas that separate 'extra information' from main clauses of sentences are used. So, in these situations, you'd need to use a pair of dashes.

For example:

- *The beach – which was empty and serene – was her favourite place to spend time.*
- *Seoul's Olympic Park – which played host to the 1988 Olympics – was renovated in 2011.*
- *Rahul – my cousin – graduated from university this summer.*

While this usage of the dash seems interchangeable with the commas mentioned above, they convey a slightly different meaning or connotation. Namely, the choice to use dashes instead of commas in a situation like this would be the choice to write a more emphatic sentence.

In other words, if the 'extra information' you wish to include within your sentence is more important, or you wish to draw more attention to it, perhaps you'd prefer the use of dashes (over commas) to contain it. In creative writing, this is certainly something to experiment with. When writing dialogue, for example, a pair of dashes could be used when you wish your character to go off track in the middle of a sentence before resuming.

For example:

- *"I'm very angry with you – I'll deal with Maurice later – you're in so much trouble."*

- *"Mrs. Haverley is fully booked all week — I need to tell Mason, actually — please don't bother her."*

- *"As you can see, the River Nile stretches from — Jeff, stop talking — all the way down in Uganda, through the continent, and up into the Mediterranean Sea."*

However, in most situations, you should stick to using commas to separate extra information like this in a sentence. The use of dashes in this way could even be considered incorrect if the extra information does not represent a clear enough interruption of the sentence.

Crafting Sentences

Now that we've shown you how to craft a sentence, let's dive into what makes a 'good sentence', and what you should be aiming for when writing under formal conditions.

A good starting point would be to think about the length of your sentences. In many cases, you should aim to keep your sentences as short as possible. This is not for word count-related reasons, but to keep your sentences concise and focused. Essentially, it ensures you are not writing 'empty' sentences or waffling.

Of course, in creative writing, such a hard-and-fast rule could stymie your voice or stifle a particular mood that you were aiming to create. In these cases, don't let ruthless efficiency get in the way of your style.

So, let's have a look at how you can cut the excess words from your sentences.

For example:

- *Without question, it is possible to say that the Fool has an important role to play in the plot of King Lear. This character represents Lear's conscience throughout and, ironically, acts a foil to his foolishness.*

This could become:

- *The Fool represents Lear's conscience throughout and, ironically, acts as a foil to his foolishness.*

Avoiding repetition is an effective way to sharpen up a sentence; you don't need to say the same thing in many different ways. If you are writing an essay, repetition will not further your point or improve your work. It could even cause whoever's marking to lose interest or penalise you. You don't want to create the impression that you're fluffing up your writing to meet the word count – quite the opposite.

Make your reader feel as if every word was selected for a clear and proactive reason. If you're looking to cut down a piece of writing that's over the word limit, experiment with taking out words and phrases that could be considered as overkill. A lot of the time, you'll find that the meaning of what you're saying hasn't changed, and your writing has become punchier and more impactful.

Creating Paragraphs

In this section, we're going to look beyond creating sentences and look at how best to weave them together to craft paragraphs. Luckily, in academic or any sort of formal writing, there are clear rules you can follow to make sure that your paragraphs are concise, focused, and driving your point forwards. Read on for our tips on creating paragraphs.

Paragraph Structure

In academic writing or essay writing, it is extremely important to write good paragraphs. A good paragraph is one that is contained, and one that does not contain lots of complex points.

As a rule, you should try and keep paragraphs limited to one main point. This way, you can stop paragraphs from growing out of control, allowing the reader to understand your argument more easily.

A great way to make your paragraphs easier to follow is to treat each of them as a miniature essay. By this, we mean that each paragraph should have a short sentence which introduces the main point, followed by the point itself. Finally, you should end the paragraph with a short sentence which briefly summarises your point, and demonstrates how it relates to the question that you're answering. This way, you'll have your argument for each paragraph clearly laid out for the reader to see.

If it helps, you can try coming up with a subtitle for each paragraph in your essay. Don't include this in the finished copy, but writing each paragraph with the main point of it explicitly in mind will help you focus your efforts, and create a more consistent piece of work.

Once you have a paragraph structure laid out, the flow of your essay will become a lot more pronounced. This means that you'll be able to spot parts that feel disjointed and correct their course. By 'disjointed', we mean parts of the essay which either stick out from the flow of your essay and don't lead to any new points, or sections which actively move against the flow of your essay.

Imagine your essay is a river. Each part of the essay should flow into the next, as your argument cumulatively builds up towards the conclusion. The points made in earlier paragraphs should always contribute to later ones, and those which don't could be considered as irrelevant.

For example, if paragraphs A, B, C, and D all support a larger argument made in paragraph F, but the argument in paragraph E has no bearing on this argument, then you need to consider whether it's paying off for you. If the paragraph isn't benefitting your argument, then you should probably get rid of it and use the space to write something relevant.

There's no set length that a paragraph needs to be, but they can be too long. If you have a single paragraph that's significantly larger than the rest in your essay, it might be worth revisiting to see how it can be divided into smaller parts. This will prevent your essay from becoming 'bogged down'. Likewise, lots of tiny paragraphs can look too fragmented or poorly developed.

IELTS Academic Writing: Task 1

As we explained in the previous chapter, task 1 will require you to look at an image, and then construct an explanation about what you see.

In this chapter, we'll show you exactly how to do this, and provide you with loads of practice questions!

Let's start out by looking at an example:

Practice Question 1

The graph below shows the relationship between shoplifting incidents and the time of year, in Scotland, Ireland and England.

Summarise the information by selecting and identifying the main features of the graph.

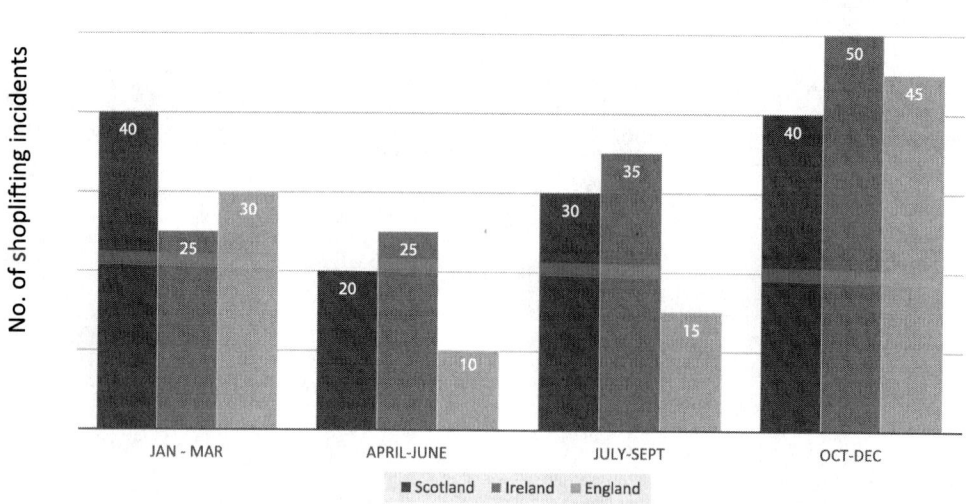

How To Answer

Sometimes, looking at a graph can seem quite intimidating. There's a lot of information to take in, and it can be quite hard to make sense of it all. The thing to do here is to stay composed. Don't panic and let the information overwhelm you. Take a moment just to look at everything in a calm and logical fashion, and work out exactly what the graph is showing. Once you've done that, your answer shouldn't be too difficult. All you have to do is summarise exactly what you see in the graph, in 150 words or more.

So, how should we look at the above graph? The first thing that should stand out for you is that the graph shows the relationship between the months of the year and the number of shoplifting incidents that occurred, in the countries of Scotland, Ireland and England. Your first line should explain this. So:

'The graph shows a correlation between the time of the year and the number of shoplifting incidents that occur in the countries of Scotland, Ireland and England.'

Now that you've summarised the main point of the graph, you can move onto the actual data. When we look at this graph, we can clearly see that there are more shoplifting incidents occurring from January-March, and October-December, than there are from April-June and July-September. Therefore, logic would dictate that more shoplifting incidents are occurring during the colder months of the year.

Once you've established this, you just need to work out the numbers behind the increase/decrease, and then summarise this. Like so:

'By looking at this graph, we can see a clear indication that more shoplifting incidents occur during the 'colder' months of the year than during the hotter months. To demonstrate this, the graph shows that from January to March (in all three countries) there were 95 shoplifting incidents in total. This was followed by a marked decrease, with only 135 incidents occurring over the next 6 months. It is worth noting that there was an increase in shoplifting incidents from July till September, compared to April till June, but this was quite a minor leap.'

In the above we've covered the first 9 months of the year. Now we can close our summary by detailing the final 3 months of the year:

'Following this, and moving into the Autumn, we saw a large increase in the number of incidents – with 135 incidents occurring over the next 3 months, from October till December.'

If we put this altogether, we have a concise, accurate and 150+ word summary of the graph in question:

'The graph shows a correlation between the time of the year and the number of shoplifting incidents that occur in the countries of Scotland, Ireland and England.

By looking at this graph, we can see a clear indication that more shoplifting incidents occur during the 'colder' months of the year than during the hotter months. To demonstrate this, the graph shows that from January to March (in all three countries) there were 95 shoplifting incidents in total. This was followed by a marked decrease, with only 135 incidents occurring over the next 6 months. It is worth noting that there was an increase in shoplifting incidents from July till September, compared to April till June, but this was quite a minor leap.

Following this, and moving into the Autumn, we saw a large increase in the number of incidents – with 135 incidents occurring over the next 3 months, from October till December.'

Now, let's look at another type of question, this time involving a diagram.

Practice Question 2

The diagram shows an ocean food chain. In your own words, describe this food chain and how it works.

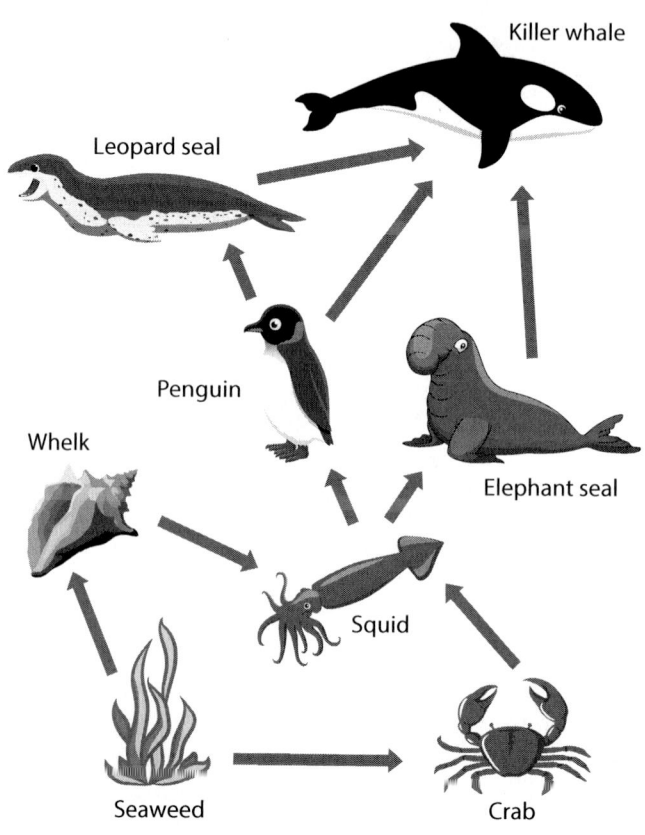

How To Answer

This is a very different type of question to the previous, in that it doesn't contain large amounts of data. However, there's still plenty of information here with which to construct a great response.

Just like before, let's start out by summarising exactly what we can see in the diagram:

'This diagram shows an aquatic food chain. In the diagram we can see a number of aquatic species, ranging from killer whales to squid.'

So, now that we've summarised the main point of the diagram, we can start exploring the details. This is quite a simple one – all you need to do is explain what eats what!

'The aquatic food chain shows which animals are higher and lower in the natural order of predator and prey. To start off with, we have seaweed. Seaweed is at the very bottom of the scale, and is consumed by both crabs and whelks. The next lowest creatures on the chain are the crab and whelk. Both the crab and whelk eat seaweed, but are consumed by squid. Squid have two main predators, the penguin and the elephant seal. The penguin is prey for the leopard seal, plus killer whales. Likewise, the elephant seal is also eaten by killer whales, who also consume leopard seals.'

Now, close out the summary with a conclusory statement:

'Based on the diagram, the killer whale is clearly the apex predator of this food chain. The killer whale does not have any predators.'

Put this all together, and we have a 152-word summary, that clearly and concisely explains what is happening in the diagram:

'This diagram shows an aquatic food chain. In the diagram we can see a number of aquatic species, ranging from killer whales to squid.

The aquatic food chain shows which animals are higher and lower in the natural order of predator and prey. To start off with, we have seaweed. Seaweed is at the very bottom of the scale, and is consumed by both crabs and whelks. The next lowest creatures on the chain are the crab and whelk. Both the crab and whelk eat seaweed, but are consumed by squid. Squid have two main predators, the penguin and the elephant seal. The penguin is prey for the leopard seal, plus killer whales. Likewise, the elephant seal is also eaten by killer whales, who also consume leopard seals.

Based on the diagram, the killer whale is clearly the apex predator of this food chain. The killer whale does not have any predators.'

Now let's do one more practice question, before we move onto some actual tests.

Practice Question 3

The table below shows the number of people who did sport, at school and university, and their gender.

Summarise the information by selecting and identifying the main features of the table.

Type of establishment	Secondary School		University	
	Male	Female	Male	Female
Football	256	62	398	162
Dance	165	268	169	368
Boxing	13	3	358	123
Tennis	98	68	160	76
Rounders	16	68	26	43
Total =	548	469	1111	772

Football = 878
Dance = 970
Boxing = 497
Tennis = 402
Rounders = 153

How To Answer

So, in this question instead of having a graph or a diagram, we now have a table, with the numbers and data filled in for us. Just like before, we need to start off the answer by summarising what the main point of the table is:

'The table shows the number of male and female athletes in secondary school, for 5 different sports, and then compares them against the number of male and female athletes at university, for the same sports.'

Now that we've summarised the main point of the table, we can move onto the smaller details – the numerical implications of the table.

'The table is broken down into individual sports – football, dance, boxing, tennis and rounders. It is also broken down to show how many of each gender participated in each sport. There are some clear differentials here, which show that certain sports are more popular amongst certain genders. For example, across both secondary school and university there were 654 boys who played football, compared to just 224 girls who played football. Both dance and boxing also contain large differentials, with dance weighted at 636 female participants to 334 male participants, and boxing weighted at 371 male participants to 126 female participants. The other sports, tennis and rounders, were more evenly spread.'

Sometimes, the table or data that you'll be given will contain lots of information. It would be impossible to summarise every single part of the above table in just 150 words, so your main aim should be to write as concisely as possible about the main elements of the table. In this case, we've identified the large differential between males and females in certain sports. However, you could also have identified the significant increase in the overall number of people who participated in sports at university, compared to that of secondary school, as the main point of the table.

Now, close out the summary with a conclusion:

'The table clearly indicates that there are certain sports which lean heavily towards male or female preference, whereas there are others which don't garner the same level of gender bias.'

Put this all together, and we have a 175-word summary, that accurately describes the table:

'The table shows the number of male and female athletes in secondary school, for 5 different sports, and then compares them against the number of male and female athletes at university, for the same sports.'

The table is broken down into individual sports – football, dance, boxing, tennis and rounders. It is also broken down to show how many of each gender participated in each sport. There are some clear differentials here, which show that certain sports are more popular amongst certain genders. For example, across both secondary school and university there were 654 boys who played football, compared to just 224 girls who played football. Both dance and boxing also contain large differentials, with dance weighted at 636 female participants to 334 male participants, and boxing weighted at 371 male participants to 126 female participants. The other sports, tennis and rounders, were more evenly spread.

'The table clearly indicates that there are certain sports which lean heavily towards male or female preference, whereas there are others which don't garner the same level of gender bias.'

Now that we've given you a good idea of how to tackle these types of exercises, it's time for you to have a go at some questions yourself.

In the next chapter we've included a range of sample questions, all similar to the above. This should give you plenty of practice!

Task 1: Practice Questions

IELTS Academic Writing 8+

Q1. The table below shows holiday preferences for Spain, America and the UK. Summarise the data in the table, in 150 words or more.

Holiday Preferences	Abroad				In the UK			
	Spain		America		Butlins		Lake District	
	Couples	Families	Couples	Families	Couples	Families	Couples	Families
All inclusive	103	208	287	316	12	176	68	109
Half board	216	233	187	84	6	164	52	68
Self Service	36	95	79	65	1	76	36	49
Total =	355	536	553	465	19	416	156	226

Total no. holidays = 2726

All inclusive = 1279
Half Board = 1010
Self Service = 437

Task 1: Practice Questions 37

Q2. The diagram below shows a common food web. Describe this food web, in 150 words or more.

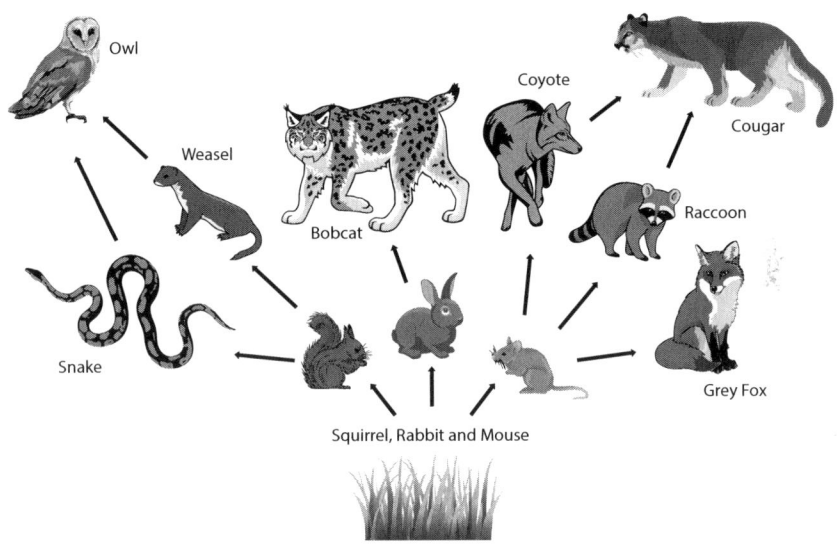

IELTS Academic Writing 8+

Q3. The diagram below shows a plant. Describe this diagram, in 150 words or more.

Rain falls from clouds, giving soil moisture.

Finally, the leaves and flower receive the water they need.

Then, the stem sucks up the water from the roots.

First, the roots absorb water from the soil.

Q4. The graph below shows the number of films released over the course of a year. Summarise the data in 150 words or more.

No. of films released and the genre

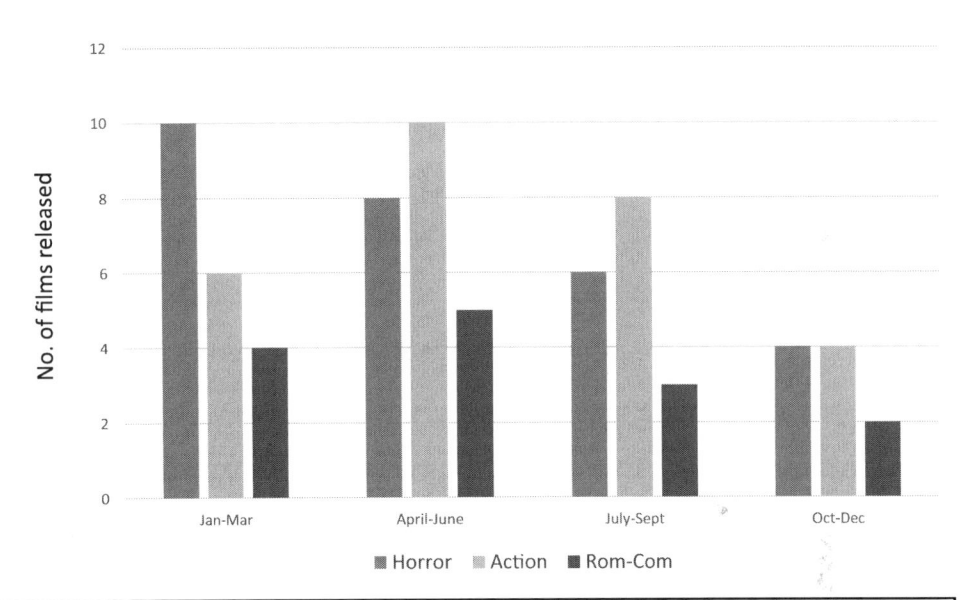

40 IELTS Academic Writing 8+

Q5. The image below shows various states of matter. Summarise the information in 150 words or more.

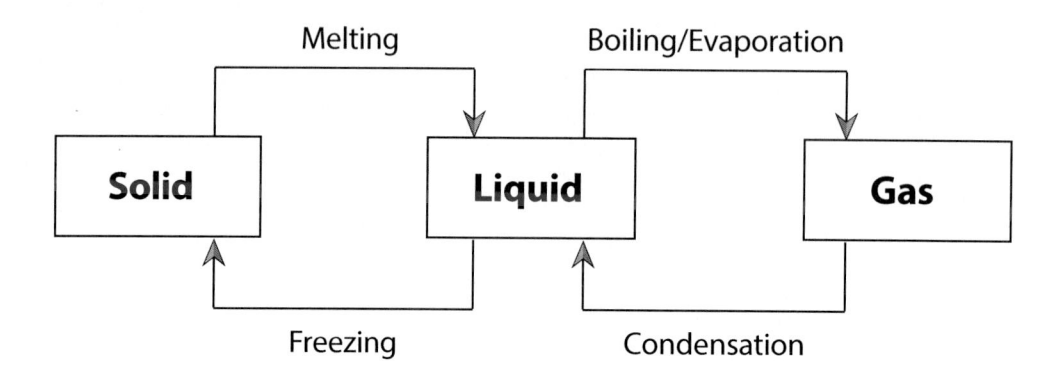

```
                Melting                    Boiling/Evaporation
        ┌─────────────────┐         ┌─────────────────────┐
        │                 ▼         │                     ▼
   ┌─────────┐        ┌─────────┐              ┌─────────┐
   │  Solid  │        │ Liquid  │              │   Gas   │
   └─────────┘        └─────────┘              └─────────┘
        ▲                 ▲         │                     │
        └─────────────────┘         └─────────────────────┘
                Freezing                    Condensation
```

Q6. The table below shows various careers in England, Scotland, Ireland and Wales. Summarise the data in 150 words or more.

Job Occupation	England Male	England Female	Scotland Male	Scotland Female	Ireland Male	Ireland Female	Wales Male	Wales Female
Police officer	165	251	150	76	30	26	45	13
Teacher	98	208	96	120	23	64	36	65
Musician	206	121	126	35	169	13	76	9
Doctor	365	68	43	35	46	26	16	15
Sales	156	65	56	32	54	18	62	36
Total =	990	713	471	298	322	147	235	138

Grand Total = 3314
No. of Police officers = 756
No. of Teachers = 710
No. of Musicians = 755
No. of Doctors = 614
No. of Sales = 479

Q7. The diagram below shows the water cycle. Summarise the information in 150 words or more.

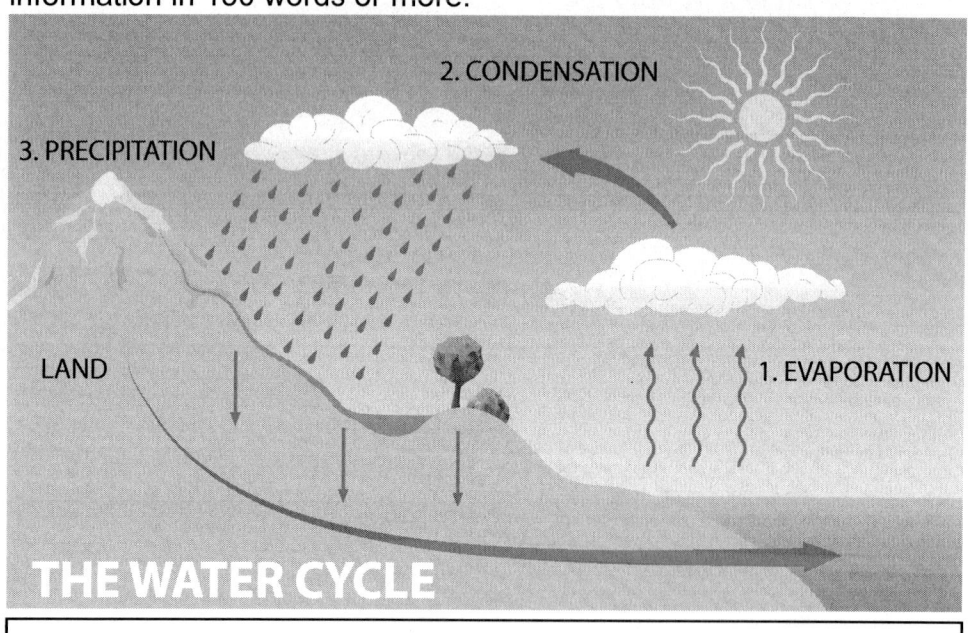

THE WATER CYCLE

1. EVAPORATION
2. CONDENSATION
3. PRECIPITATION
LAND

Task 1: Practice Questions 43

Q8. The table shows the number of English papers published by top UK universities over a six-year period. Summarise the data in 150 words or more.

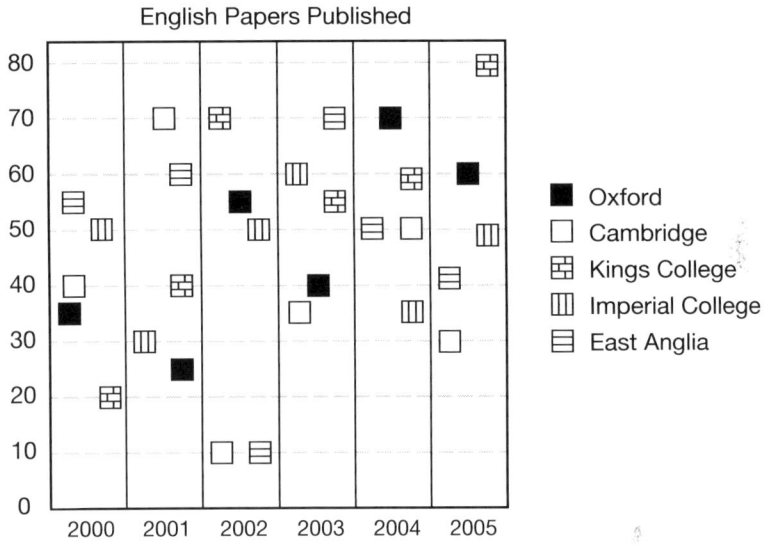

English Papers Published

- ■ Oxford
- □ Cambridge
- ⊞ Kings College
- ⏢ Imperial College
- ⊟ East Anglia

Q9. The table shows pregnancy rates and decisions for the countries of England, Italy, Spain and Wales. Summarise the data in 150 words or more.

Location	Teenage pregnancy regarding location							
	England		Italy		Spain		Wales	
	13-16	17-20	13-16	17-20	13-16	17-20	13-16	17-20
Keeping the baby	36	63	11	23	19	23	2	3
Abortion	12	13	6	13	16	3	0	1
Adoption	16	16	8	9	4	5	1	1
Undecided	43	23	16	11	18	19	1	2
Total =	107	115	41	56	57	50	4	7

Total no. of pregnancies = 437
England = 222
Italy = 97
Spain = 107
Wales = 11

Task 1: Practice Questions 45

Q10. The table below shows the scores for students in English, Maths and Science examinations. Summarise the data in 150 words or more.

Subject	Marks out of 40			
	30 and above	20 and above	10 and above	0 and above
English	19	52	91	100
Maths	13	36	90	100
Science	11	42	87	100
AVERAGE	14	43	89	100

Q11. The image below shows information related to breast cancer. Summarise the information in this image in 150 words or more.

BREAST CANCER INFOGRAPHIC

1 IN 8 WOMAN DIAGNOSED WITH BREAST CANCER

The dynamics of the incidence of breast cancer (2000–2015)

2000 2005 2010 2015

RISK FACTORS
- NOT BREASTFEEDING
- LATE PREGNANCY
- STRESS
- AIR POLLUTION
- LACK OF SLEEP
- EXCESS BODYFAT
- FEMALE GENDER
- FAMILY HISTORY
- RADIATION EXPOSURE

HOW TO REDUCE RISK
- Don't smoke
- Drink less alcohol
- Do regular exercise
- Have regular mammograms

48 IELTS Academic Writing 8+

Q12. The image below shows information related to exercise. Summarise the information in this image in 150 words or more.

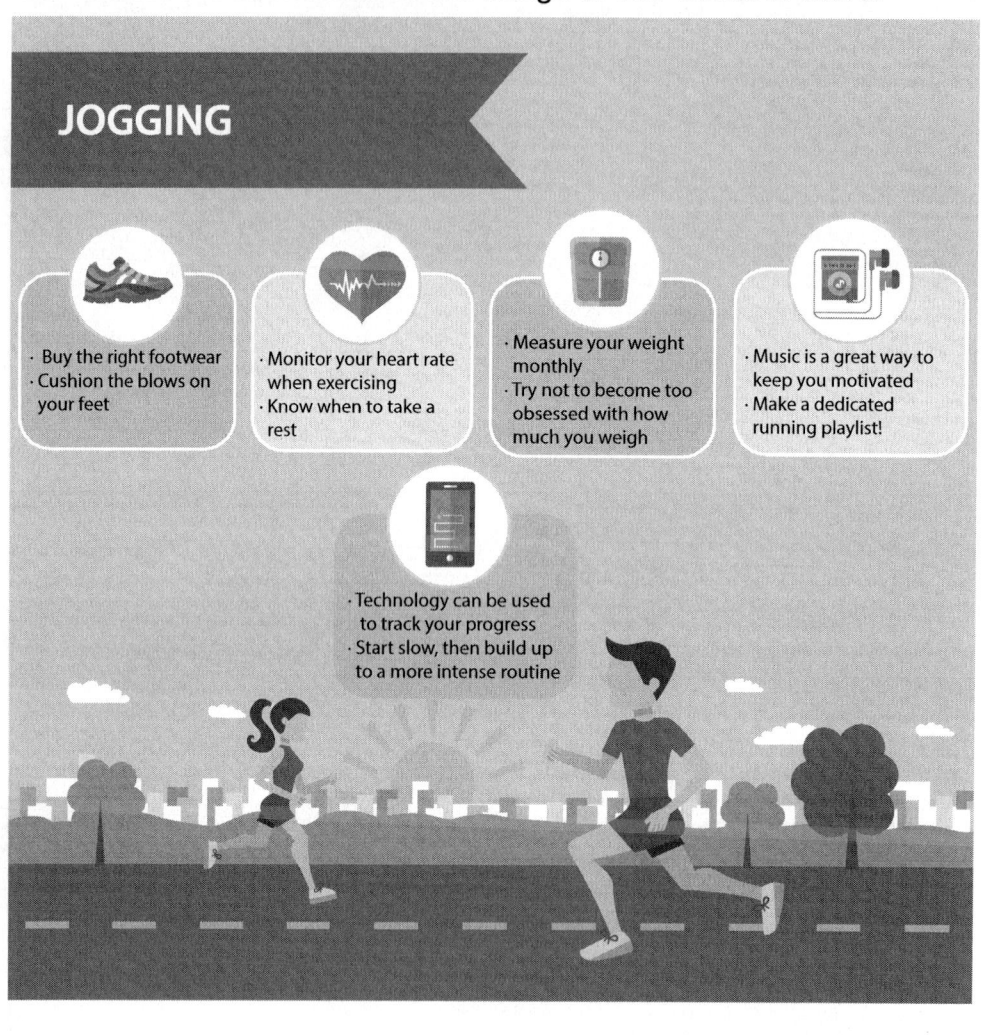

JOGGING

- Buy the right footwear
- Cushion the blows on your feet

- Monitor your heart rate when exercising
- Know when to take a rest

- Measure your weight monthly
- Try not to become too obsessed with how much you weigh

- Music is a great way to keep you motivated
- Make a dedicated running playlist!

- Technology can be used to track your progress
- Start slow, then build up to a more intense routine

50 IELTS Academic Writing 8+

Q13. The image below shows different aspects of a car. Summarise the information in this image in 150 words or more.

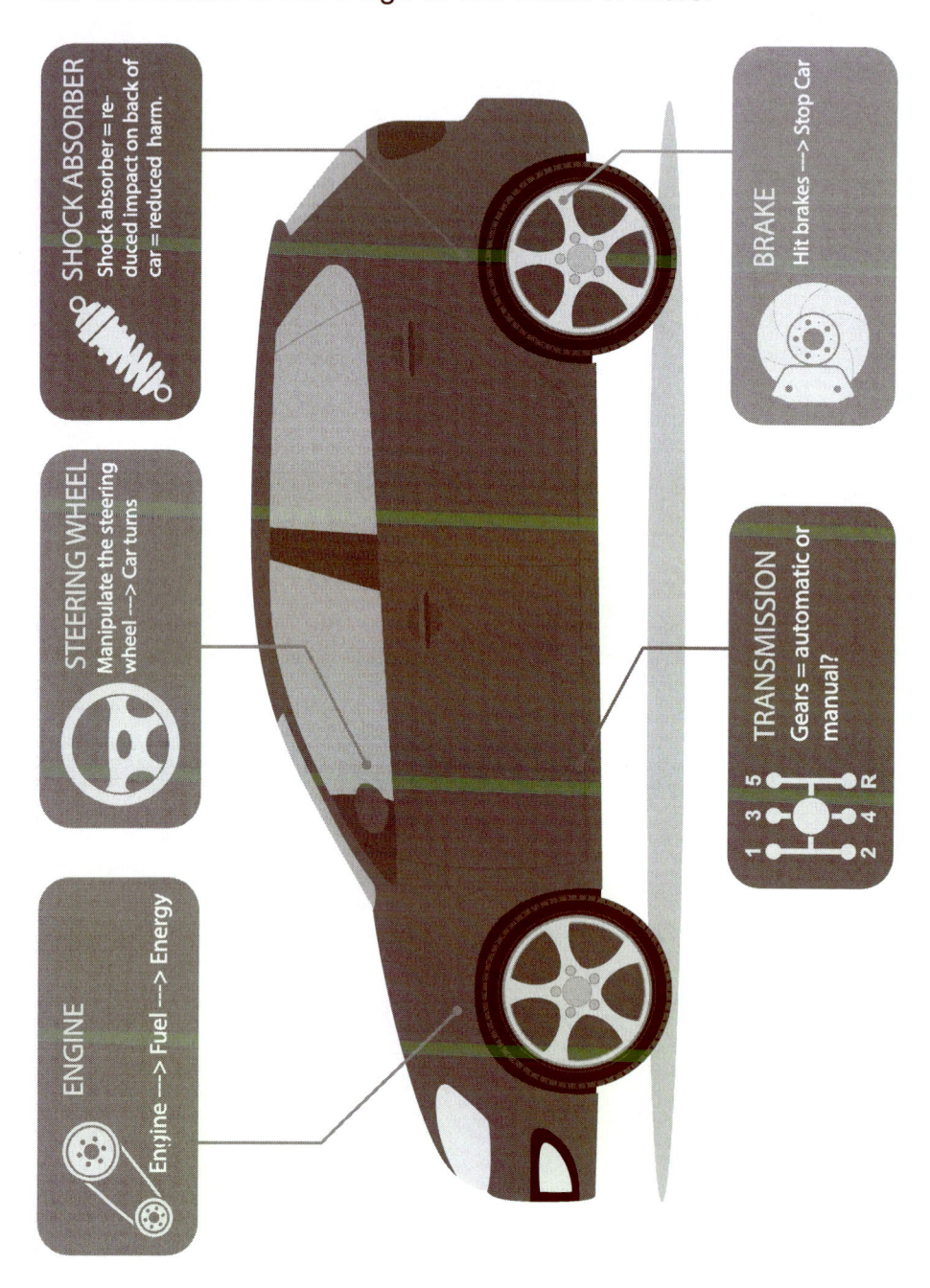

SHOCK ABSORBER
Shock absorber = reduced impact on back of car = reduced harm.

BRAKE
Hit brakes —> Stop Car

STEERING WHEEL
Manipulate the steering wheel —> Car turns

TRANSMISSION
Gears = automatic or manual?

ENGINE
Engine —> Fuel —> Energy

IELTS Academic Writing 8+

Q14. The image below shows worldwide and American pizza preferences. Summarise the information in this image in 150 words or more.

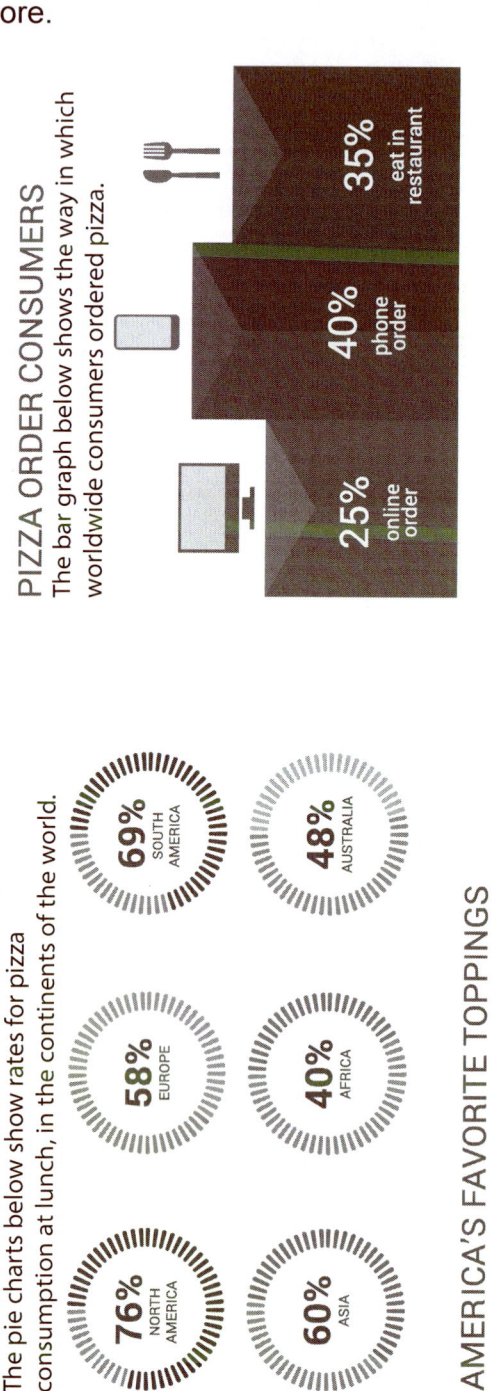

PIZZA ORDER CONSUMERS

The bar graph below shows the way in which worldwide consumers ordered pizza.

- 35% eat in restaurant
- 40% phone order
- 25% online order

PIZZA CONSUMPTION AT LUNCH

The pie charts below show rates for pizza consumption at lunch, in the continents of the world.

- NORTH AMERICA: 76%
- SOUTH AMERICA: 69%
- EUROPE: 58%
- ASIA: 60%
- AFRICA: 40%
- AUSTRALIA: 48%

AMERICA'S FAVORITE TOPPINGS

The figures below show percentage statistics for America's favourite flavour of pizza.

- PEPPERONI: 41.5%
- CHEESE: 15.9%
- MUSHROOMS: 11.5%
- SAUSAGE: 4.1%
- CHICKEN: 3.9%
- BACON: 2.5%
- PINEAPPLE: 8.4%
- OTHER: 11.4%

Q15. The image below shows dietary recommendations for dogs. Summarise the information in this image in 150 words or more.

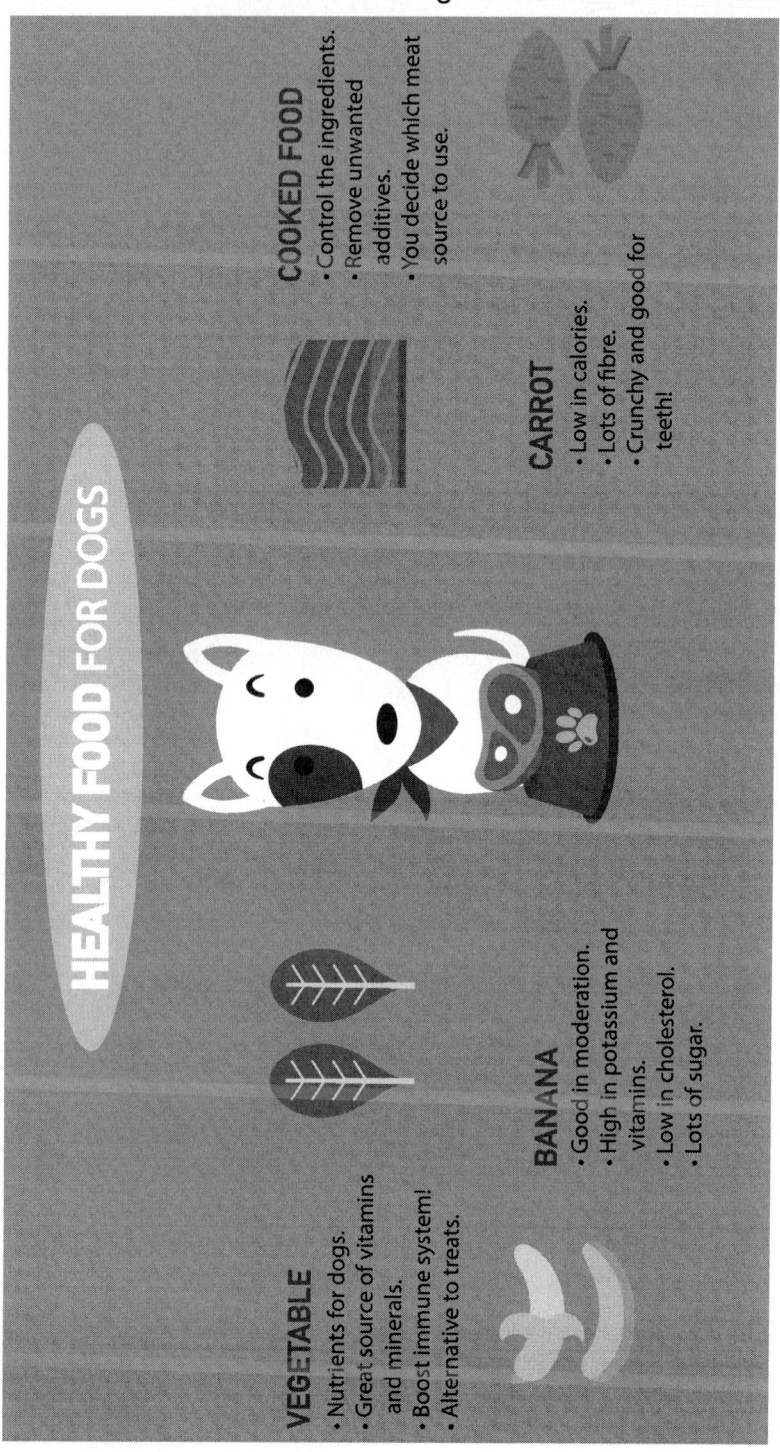

HEALTHY FOOD FOR DOGS

COOKED FOOD
- Control the ingredients.
- Remove unwanted additives.
- You decide which meat source to use.

CARROT
- Low in calories.
- Lots of fibre.
- Crunchy and good for teeth!

VEGETABLE
- Nutrients for dogs.
- Great source of vitamins and minerals.
- Boost immune system!
- Alternative to treats.

BANANA
- Good in moderation.
- High in potassium and vitamins.
- Low in cholesterol.
- Lots of sugar.

56 IELTS Academic Writing 8+

Q16. The image below shows various tips for exam preparation. Summarise the information in this image in 150 words or more.

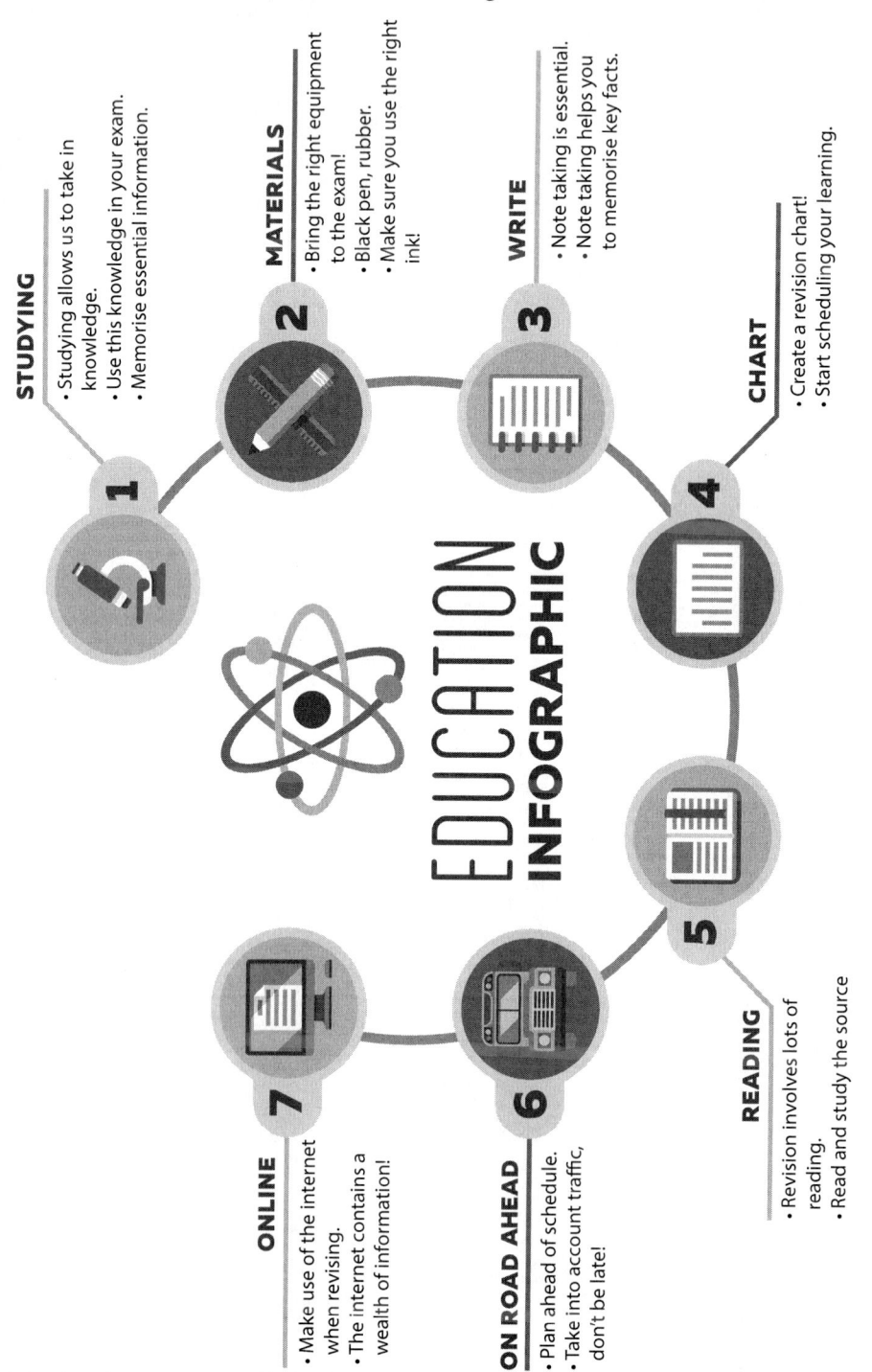

EDUCATION INFOGRAPHIC

1. STUDYING
- Studying allows us to take in knowledge.
- Use this knowledge in your exam.
- Memorise essential information.

2. MATERIALS
- Bring the right equipment to the exam!
- Black pen, rubber.
- Make sure you use the right ink!

3. WRITE
- Note taking is essential.
- Note taking helps you to memorise key facts.

4. CHART
- Create a revision chart!
- Start scheduling your learning.

5. READING
- Revision involves lots of reading.
- Read and study the source

6. ON ROAD AHEAD
- Plan ahead of schedule.
- Take into account traffic, don't be late!

7. ONLINE
- Make use of the internet when revising.
- The internet contains a wealth of information!

Q17. The image below shows information related to lung cancer. Summarise the information in this image in 150 words or more.

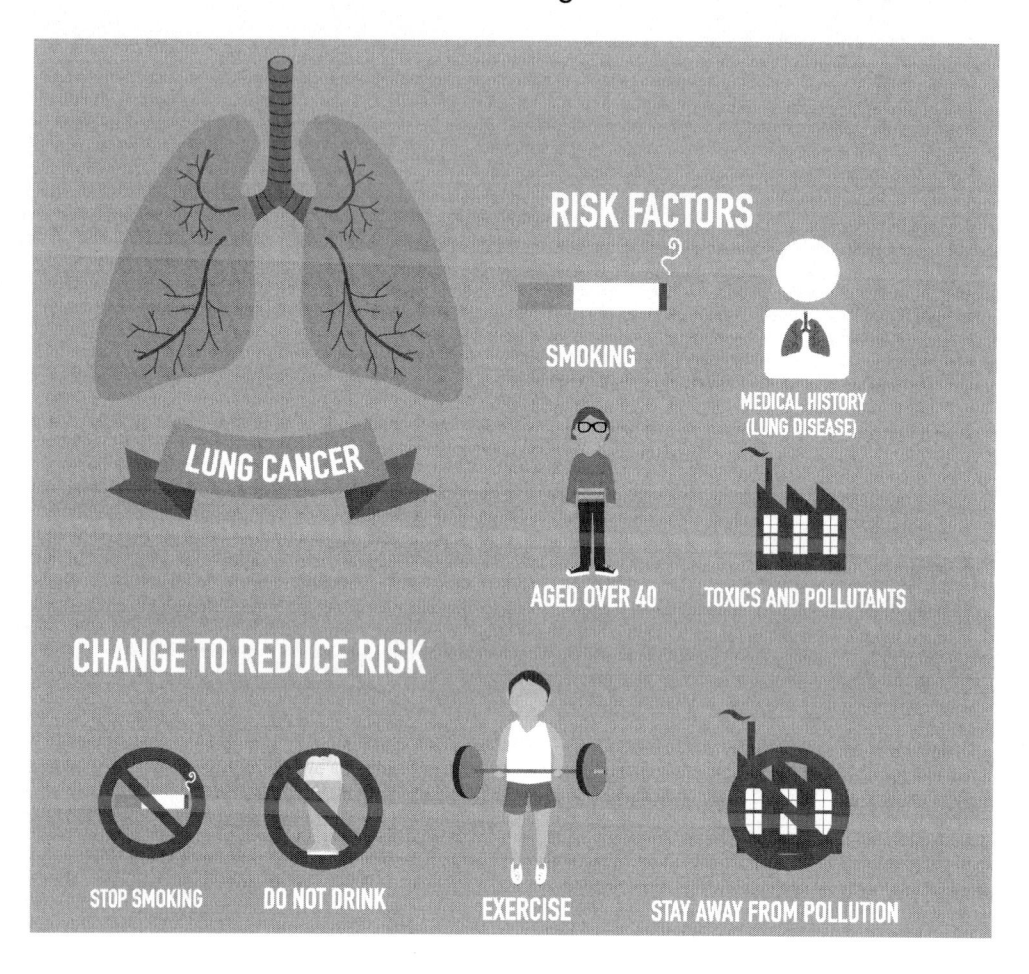

RISK FACTORS

- SMOKING
- AGED OVER 40
- MEDICAL HISTORY (LUNG DISEASE)
- TOXICS AND POLLUTANTS

LUNG CANCER

CHANGE TO REDUCE RISK

- STOP SMOKING
- DO NOT DRINK
- EXERCISE
- STAY AWAY FROM POLLUTION

Q18. The image below shows the carbon cycle. Summarise the information in this image in 150 words or more.

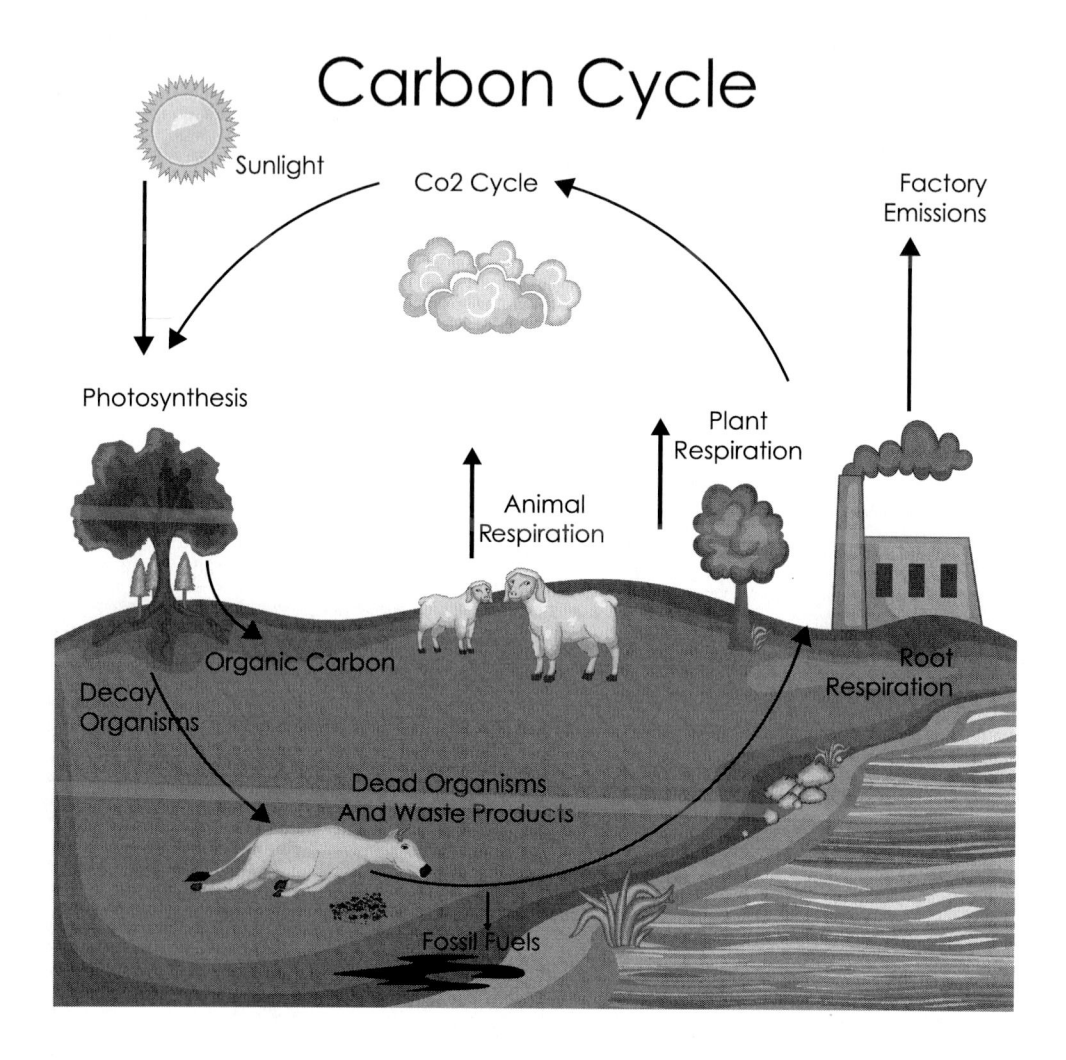

Carbon Cycle

62   **IELTS Academic Writing 8+**

Q19. The image below shows the various stages of constructing, then selling, a house. Summarise the information in 150 words or more.

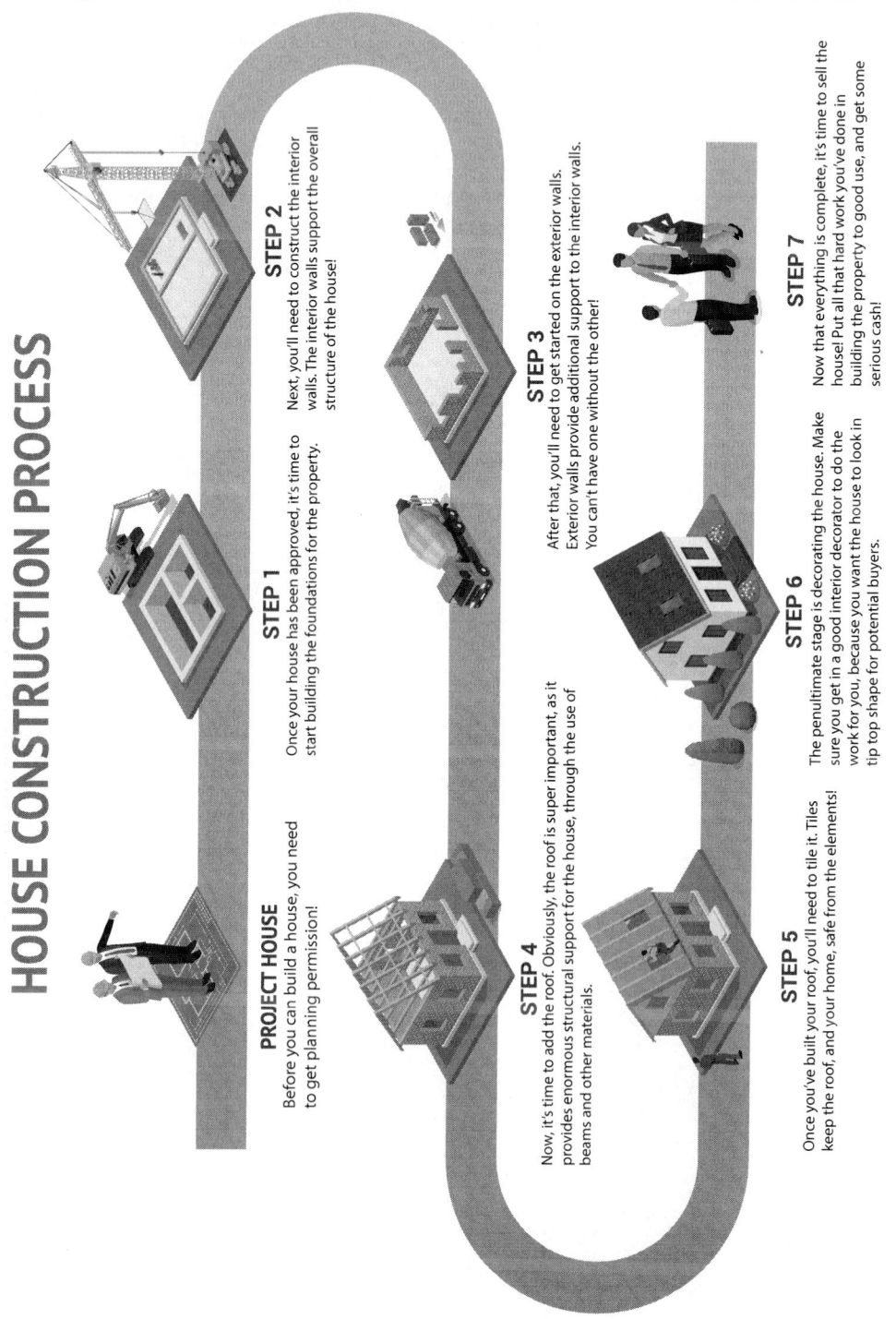

HOUSE CONSTRUCTION PROCESS

PROJECT HOUSE
Before you can build a house, you need to get planning permission!

STEP 1
Once your house has been approved, it's time to start building the foundations for the property.

STEP 2
Next, you'll need to construct the interior walls. The interior walls support the overall structure of the house!

STEP 3
After that, you'll need to get started on the exterior walls. Exterior walls provide additional support to the interior walls. You can't have one without the other!

STEP 4
Now, it's time to add the roof. Obviously, the roof is super important, as it provides enormous structural support for the house, through the use of beams and other materials.

STEP 5
Once you've built your roof, you'll need to tile it. Tiles keep the roof, and your home, safe from the elements!

STEP 6
The penultimate stage is decorating the house. Make sure you get in a good interior decorator to do the work for you, because you want the house to look in tip top shape for potential buyers.

STEP 7
Now that everything is complete, it's time to sell the house! Put all that hard work you've done in building the property to good use, and get some serious cash!

Q20. The image below shows the health benefits of lemons. Summarise the information in 150 words or more.

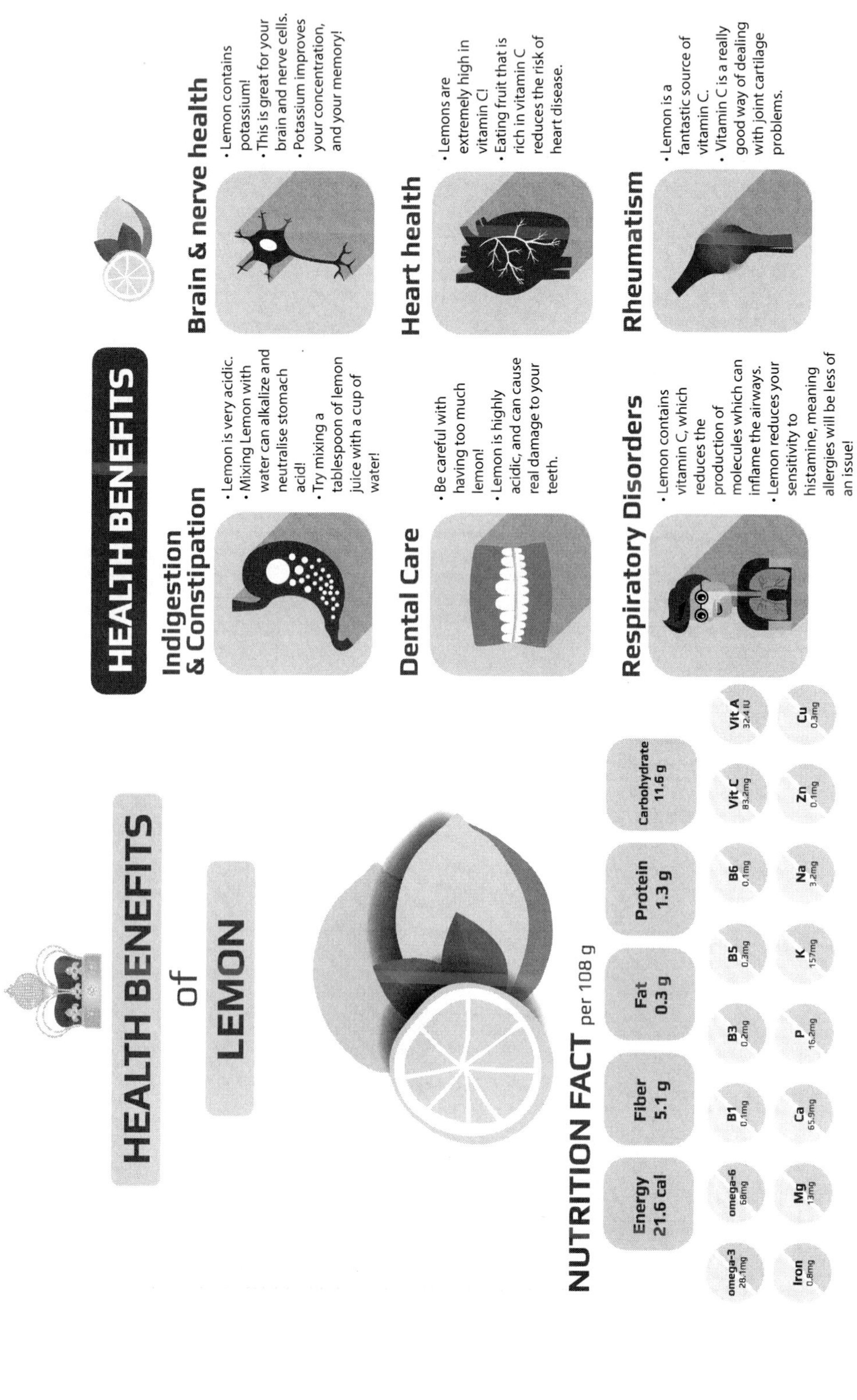

HEALTH BENEFITS of LEMON

NUTRITION FACT per 108 g

Energy	Fiber	Fat	Protein	Carbohydrate
21.6 cal	5.1 g	0.3 g	1.3 g	11.6 g

- omega-3: 28.1mg
- omega-6: 68mg
- B1: 0.1mg
- B3: 0.2mg
- B5: 0.3mg
- B6: 0.1mg
- Vit C: 83.2mg
- Vit A: 32.4 IU
- Iron: 0.8mg
- Mg: 13mg
- Ca: 65.9mg
- P: 16.2mg
- K: 157mg
- Na: 3.2mg
- Zn: 0.1mg
- Cu: 0.3mg

HEALTH BENEFITS

Brain & nerve health
- Lemon contains potassium!
- This is great for your brain and nerve cells.
- Potassium improves your concentration, and your memory!

Heart health
- Lemons are extremely high in vitamin C!
- Eating fruit that is rich in vitamin C reduces the risk of heart disease.

Rheumatism
- Lemon is a fantastic source of vitamin C.
- Vitamin C is a really good way of dealing with joint cartilage problems.

Indigestion & Constipation
- Lemon is very acidic.
- Mixing Lemon with water can alkalize and neutralise stomach acid!
- Try mixing a tablespoon of lemon juice with a cup of water!

Dental Care
- Be careful with having too much lemon!
- Lemon is highly acidic, and can cause real damage to your teeth.

Respiratory Disorders
- Lemon contains vitamin C, which reduces the production of molecules which can inflame the airways.
- Lemon reduces your sensitivity to histamine, meaning allergies will be less of an issue!

Q21. The image below shows the process of ordering goods online. Summarise the information in 150 words or more.

SHOPPING

PRODUCT
- The final stage is for the customer to receive their product.
- Once the customer receives their product, they are often invited to leave an honest review of the company and the service they received.
- If a customer does not like the product, they are entitled to utilise the 14-day refund policy.

STEP 04

DELIVERY
- The courier will have a set number of addresses to visit
- Customers can normally track their goods using a unique tracking number
- Every customer will be assigned a delivery slot, starting from 9am, going until 5pm.

STEP 03

GOODS
- If a customer orders online, the first thing that happens is that the goods are packed ready for delivery.
- Someone from the store needs to run a detailed check, to make sure all the orders for delivery are correct.
- Once that's done, the goods are loaded out onto a van for delivery.

STEP 02

STORE
- Goods are sent from the warehouse to the store directly
- When the goods arrive at the store, they are separated into two categories: delivery and front of house product
- Customers can come into the store, or they can order online!

STEP 01

Q22. The image below shows conviction and crime rates for adults and people aged under 21. Summarise the information in 150 words or more.

	Convicted				Non-Convicted			
	Male		Female		Male		Female	
	A	U21	A	U21	A	U21	A	U21
Theft	166	265	68	96	46	26	24	15
Drug Offences	356	254	126	85	12	4	4	3
Motoring	369	369	49	109	56	65	31	45
Criminal Damage	256	251	169	56	43	15	2	13
Sexual Offences	235	96	19	10	5	3	2	1
Fraud	357	23	120	8	13	11	16	10
Total =	1739	1258	551	364	175	124	79	87

Grand Total = 4377

Convictions = 3912
Non Convictions = 465

Task 1: Practice Questions **69**

Q23. The image below shows musical preferences, for people aged 10 and upwards. Summarise the information in 150 words or more.

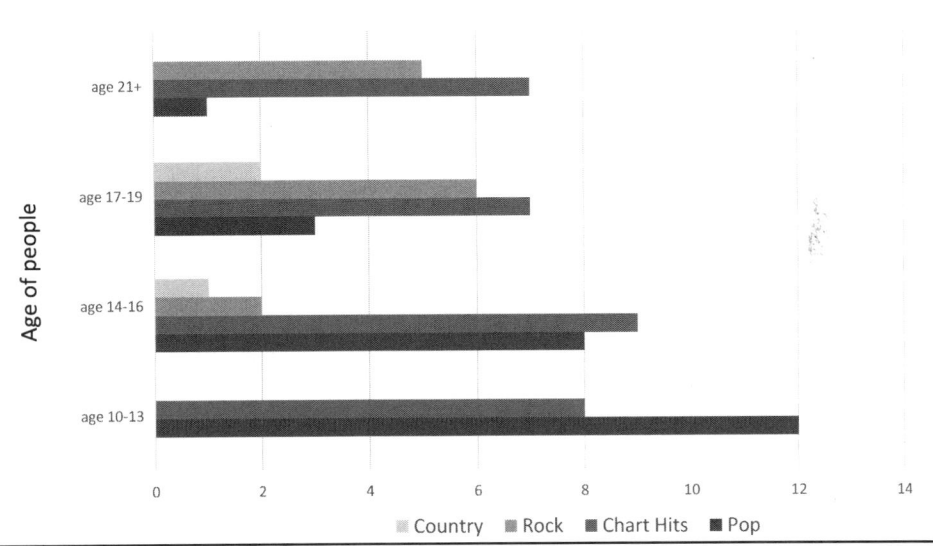

Music preferences

- Age of people
  - age 21+
  - age 17-19
  - age 14-16
  - age 10-13

0 2 4 6 8 10 12 14

■ Country ■ Rock ■ Chart Hits ■ Pop

70 IELTS Academic Writing 8+

Q24. The image below shows children's favourite animals, with participants given the choice between dog, cat and hamster. Summarise the information in 150 words or more.

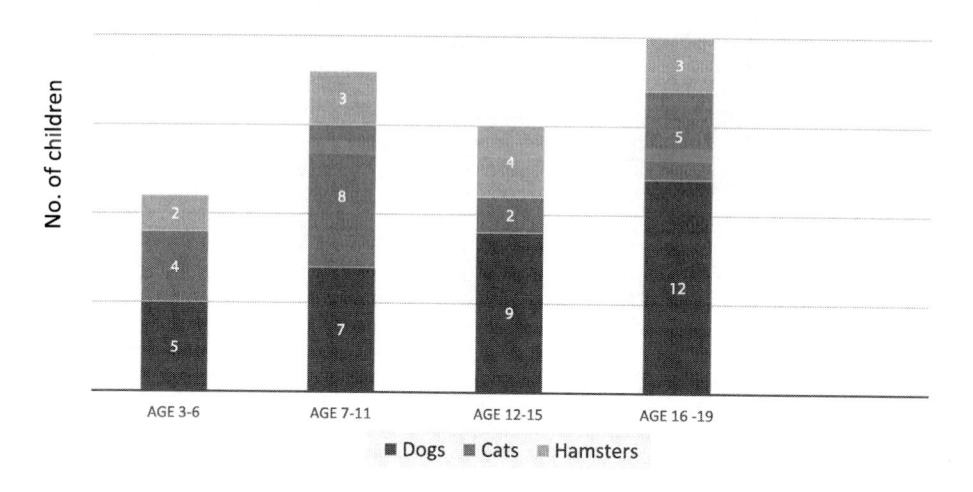

Children's favourite animals

Age group	Dogs	Cats	Hamsters
AGE 3-6	5	4	2
AGE 7-11	7	8	3
AGE 12-15	9	2	4
AGE 16-19	12	5	3

Task 1: Practice Questions

Q25. The pie chart below shows the percentage of students in each GCSE subject at a local secondary school and the number of non-US students in the subject of Geography. There were 118 students total, in Geography.

Summarise the information in 150 words or more.

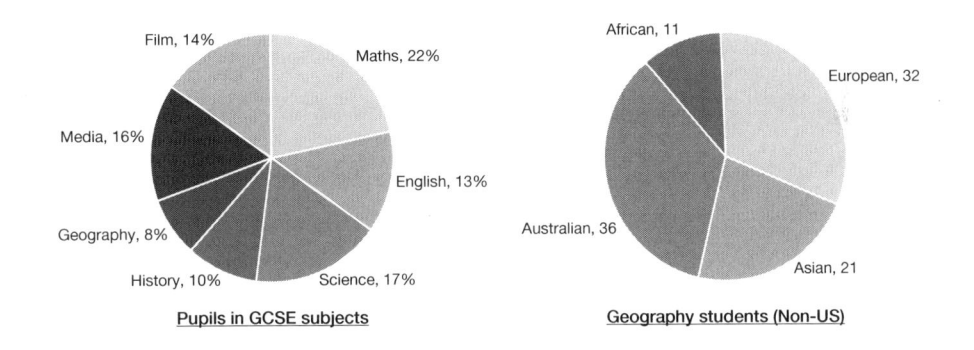

Pupils in GCSE subjects
- Maths, 22%
- Film, 14%
- Media, 16%
- Geography, 8%
- History, 10%
- Science, 17%
- English, 13%

Geography students (Non-US)
- African, 11
- European, 32
- Australian, 36
- Asian, 21

Task 1: Answers

74 IELTS Academic Writing 8+

Q1.

The table shows holiday preferences for tourists in Spain, America, and the UK. The table is broken up into three types of service: all inclusive, half board, and self service. The tourists themselves are also divided into two categories: couples and families.

By looking at this table, we can see a clear pattern emerging in certain categories. For a start, it is evident that holidays abroad are a far more popular choice than holidays in the UK. This is shown by the numbers of people visiting Spain and America, 891 and 1018 respectively, compared to the numbers of people visiting UK based holiday destinations, with Butlins having 435 total visitors, and the Lake District having 382 total visitors. Along with this, it is apparent that self-service is by far the least popular choice board basis. There were only 437 total self-service bookings, compared to 1279 all-inclusive, and 1010 half-board. This applies irrespective of the destination.

With the exception of trips to America, family holidays were more popular across the board, with Butlins being the best demonstration of this.

Q2.

The diagram shows a complex food web, with multiple top apex predators, and several mid-level predators.

At the bottom of the chain we have grass. This is consumed by the squirrel, rabbit, and mouse. All three of the aforementioned are prey to a number of animals, both mid-web predators and apex predators alike. The squirrel is eaten by the snake and the weasel, both of which are consumed by the owl. The rabbit is eaten by the bobcat – which has no predators. The mouse is eaten by the coyote and the racoon, both of which are eaten by the cougar. The cougar has no predators, and is therefore an apex predator. Likewise, the mouse is also prey to the grey fox, which also has no predators.

In total, there are 4 apex predators in this web: the owl, the bobcat, the cougar and the grey fox. There are only 3 animals in the entire web who would not be considered predators – the squirrel, the rabbit and the mouse.

Q3.

This diagram shows how plants use water for nourishment, and how this helps them to grow and blossom.

The first stage in the process occurs when it rains. Rain from the clouds falls onto the ground, which provides the soil with moisture. The soil absorbs this moisture, which is then carried into the earth below the plant. A plant has multiple roots, which extend deep below the ground. These roots take the moisture from the soil, passing it on to the stem. The stem serves as a safe passage for the water, which is then passed onto the leaves. It is also passed onto the flower. The diagram indicates the way in which this is done via a series of arrows, showing the direction that the water travels in once it has been absorbed by the roots of the plant. In this diagram we can see a healthy, blooming flower – which indicates that it has received a good supply of water.

Q4.

In this graph we can see the number of films released over the course of a year. The films are sorted into three categories: Horror, action, and rom-com.

The first thing that is apparent is that there were significantly less rom-coms released than any of the other two categories. From January to March there were just 4 rom-coms, compared to 10 horror films and 6 action films. From April to June there were just 5 rom-coms, compared to 8 horror films and 10 action films. July to September saw only 3 rom-coms released, a decrease from the previous months, and December saw the lowest total number of rom-coms released – with just 2. The number of horror films released throughout the year steadily decreased, starting at 10 in the first 3 months, falling to 8 in the next 3 months, and then 6 and 4 respectively. None of the other genres showed any discernible pattern, with the numbers rising and falling in equal measure as the year progressed.

Q5.

This diagram shows a number of states of matter. Starting from the left-hand side of the image, we have a 'solid'. A solid is an object, such as a piece of meat, where the particles are closely packed together. Once melted, the particles (although still close together) will flow freely, and thus it will become a liquid. If we decide to freeze the liquid, putting the particles back into form again, then we will now have a solid.

In the middle of the diagram we have a 'liquid'. As mentioned, a liquid is a state of matter where the particles can flow freely and slide. When a liquid is heated, it boils and then evaporates – in the process of this it turns into a gas. Once a gas becomes cool enough, it will condense, which turns it back into a liquid. Thus, the cycle is complete. Using this diagram, we can clearly see that there is a direct relationship between all three states of matter – solid, liquid, and gas.

Q6.

The table shows statistics for 5 different occupations in England, Scotland, Ireland, and Wales. The occupations listed are police officer, teacher, musician, doctor and sales.

When looking at this table, the first thing we can notice is that there is a clear disparity between the number of males working in the listed professions, and the number of females. Every single country apart from Wales has at least 100 more men working in the listed professions than females, and even in Wales the total differential is 97.

In terms of individual careers, the only field in this table where women outnumber their male counterparts is in teaching. England boasts quite a high differential in this regard, with 208 female teachers to just 98 male. The biggest gender differential appears in music, where there are 577 male musicians to just 178 female. The smallest gender differential appears in police officer, where there are just 24 more males than females.

Q7.

In this scientific diagram, we can clearly see the natural process of how water is cycled back from the land into the sea, and vice versa.

To start off with, the heat from the sun evaporates water from the sea, turning it into vapour. This vapour is a gas, and it then rises from the surface of the earth and into the sky. When it reaches the sky, it cools, and therefore condenses – turning from a gas into a liquid. The liquid particles become water droplets, which eventually merge together to form clouds. Once these clouds become too heavy, the water begins to fall onto the Earth, in the form of rain. If the air is cold enough then it will fall as sleet or snow. Any water which falls as precipitation into a lake or river will eventually be carried back into the sea, where the cycle begins again.

Q8.

This table displays the quantity of English papers that were published by 5 UK universities, from 2000 until 2005.

The first thing we should notice about this table, is that there is no apparent overall trend for the rate at which papers are being published. From 2000 to 2001 there was an increase of 25 papers published annually, and this decreased in 2002. From 2002 onwards there was an increase in the numbers of papers published, but 2003-2005 saw roughly the same numbers of papers being published in each of the 3 years.

In terms of individual university trends, the highest publishing university over the 6 year period was Kings College, and the lowest publishing university over the 6 year period was Cambridge – who published just 10 papers in 2002 (joint lowest with East Anglia). Kings College led the pack by some distance, publishing in advance of 40 more English papers than the nearest competitors – Oxford and East Anglia.

Q9.

In this table we can see the statistics for teenage pregnancy in England, Italy, Spain, and Wales. The table separates those being measured by two different age groups –13-16 and 17-20, and also looks at what these people decided (or didn't decide) to do with their baby.

The first thing that we can notice when looking at this table is that in all the countries, the majority of people measured decided to keep their baby – 188 people in total opted for this choice. Both adoption and abortion performed poorly on a statistical level compared to keeping the baby. However, there were still a large number of people undecided about what to do with their baby, with 133 people in total selecting this option. The least popular option was adoption, with just 60 people from the whole 437 selecting this. In terms of pregnancies, England was by some distance the country with the highest number, with over double that of the nearest competitor – Spain. The country with the lowest number of pregnancies was Wales, with just 11.

Q10.

In this results-based table we can see examination scores for 100 pupils, in English, Maths, and Science. When looking at this table, the first thing we should notice is that the highest test score figures were achieved in English. In English, 19 pupils achieved a score of 30/40 or higher. Likewise, there were 52 pupils who achieved a score of 20/40 or higher. There was very little to separate Maths and Science. Whilst Maths outscored Science in the top bracket by just two pupils, with 13 Maths students achieving 30/40 or higher, compared to Science's 11 students achieving 30/40 or higher, there were more students in Science who achieved 20/40 or higher – with 42 in total for Science and 36 for Maths. This means that, overall, students in both Maths and Science performed almost equally well, but students' scores in these subjects were some distance behind their scores for English.

Q11.

The image shows important information about breast cancer, and how people can take steps to reduce the risk of getting this.

The image shows that 1 in 8 women are diagnosed with breast cancer. It clearly shows that from 2000 onwards, finishing in 2015, the number of breast cancer cases has sharply increased. The image shows this via a number of triangles, which get larger as the years progress. In the picture, we can see that there are a number of ways to reduce the risk of getting breast cancer. Refraining from smoking and refraining from drinking will both help. It also helps to do regular exercises, and have mammograms.

The diagram shows that there are several factors which will increase the risk of getting breast cancer. These include stress, air pollution, lack of sleep, excess body fat, family history, and being a female. On top of this, there is also a map, showing that breast cancer is spread widely across the world – and not just limited to certain areas.

Q12.

The image shows two runners, along with a series of tabs displaying information related to exercise. Each of the tabs contains information that is related to exercising.

To start off with, we have a running shoe. Your footwear is vital when exercising. Exercise places great strain on your body, and therefore you need the right footwear in order to cushion the blows, and support your feet. Next, is a heart symbol. The image shows us that monitoring your heart rate is very important when exercising. It shows how hard you are working, and tells you when you should stop and take a rest.

The third image is of a scale. The image advises that you should weigh yourself monthly, but don't become too worried or obsessed with this. After this, there is a headphone image. Music is a great way to keep you motivated whilst exercising, and you can even make a dedicated running playlist.

The final image shows a phone. Your phone can be used to track your progress. The image advises starting off slow, then building up to a more intense routine!

Q13.

This image shows the different parts of a car, and their function.

To start off with, we have the engine. The engine converts fuel into energy, which makes the car move. The engine is located at the front of the car in this image. Next, we have the steering wheel. The steering wheel can be manipulated by the driver, to make the car turn. It is located inside the car, on the driver's side of the vehicle.

Following this, we have the shock absorber. The shock absorber is there to take impacts on the back of the car, and reduce the risk of harm for the driver. Shock absorbers are located on the wheels. Next there is transmission. The transmission relates to your gears, and can be either automatic or manual. Finally, we have the brakes. The brakes are a key safety system in the car, as they allow the driver to stop!

Q14.

In this picture we can see statistics and figures related to the way in which citizens of the world consume pizza.

Starting with the top chart on the left-hand side, we can see the statistics for worldwide pizza consumption at lunch. This is divided up by continents. North America is the continent where pizza is most popularly consumed at lunch, with 76% of people surveyed claiming that this is what they ate. The next closest continent was South America, with 69% of people claiming that they ate pizza for lunch. After this there was a marked drop, with the next highest pizza consuming continent being Asia, with 60%.

The chart on upper right-hand side shows worldwide figures for the way in which people ordered their pizza. 40% of people ordered via phone, making this by far the most popular choice, with 35% of people eating in the pizza restaurant itself, and 25% ordering via the internet.

Finally, the chart at the bottom shows the statistics for the American public's favourite type of pizza. Pepperoni was the runaway leader in this respect, collecting 41.5% of the votes, with the next closest being cheese with 15.9%, and mushrooms at 11.5%. The least popular pizza type was bacon, with just 2.5% of the votes.

Q15.

The image shows a variety of foods that could be considered 'healthy' for dogs, and explains why these foods are healthy.

To start off with, we have vegetables. By adding vegetables to your dog's diet, you can ensure that they are taking in lots of nutrients. Vegetables provide vitamins and minerals, which are important for having a healthy canine. These also boost a dog's immune system. Vegetables are a great alternative to pet treats, which contain lots of calories.

Next on the list, we have bananas. Bananas are good for dogs, but only in moderation. They contain potassium and vitamins, and are low in cholesterol. Owners should be careful about feeding their dogs bananas, as bananas contain lots of sugar.

The third item on the list is home cooked food. Home cooked food has lots of advantages compared to purchased foods, in that you can control the ingredients you use, thereby removing any unwanted additives or preservatives. You can decide which meat sources are the best to use, especially if your dog has an allergy or particular needs.

Finally, we have carrots. Carrots are low in calories, and contain lots of fibre. Carrots are also good for dogs' teeth, due to their crunchy nature!

Q16.

This image provides us with a list of things to take into account when revising for exams.

First of all, we have studying. Studying is extremely important, as it allows us to take in knowledge and then use this in the examination. By studying, we memorise and learn vital information. Next on the list, is materials. In this chart, materials is referring to making sure you have the correct materials for the examination you are sitting – black pen, rubber, ruler, etc. The next item refers to writing. Writing notes down is a vital part of the revision process, and helps us to learn and memorise information. Then we have chart, and reading. Creating a revision chart is really useful, as it allows you to schedule your learning in a structured manner. In order to revise, you'll have to read and study the source material!

The next image is 'on the road', and this basically refers to making sure you plan your journey ahead of the examination. You need to account for problems like traffic, as you don't want to be late! Finally, we have 'online'. This essentially refers to making sure you make full use of the internet when revising, as it contains lots of useful tips and information.

Q17.

This image shows an infographic, relating to the causes of lung cancer, and the various risk factors.

Starting off with the risk factors, the image identifies four main risks. The first of these is smoking. Breathing toxins into your lungs naturally has an extremely harmful impact on the body, and therefore increases your risk. The second risk factor identified is whether you've had a medical history of lung disease. This makes you more susceptible to lung cancer, as your lungs are weaker. The third risk factor is being aged over 40. It is well known that as we get older, our bodies become more prone to infection or disease, and lung cancer is no exception. Finally, we have toxics and pollutants. Like cigarette smoke, toxics and pollutants in the air can be breathed in, travelling down to the lungs, where they cause harm.

The diagram also identifies ways of reducing the risk. The first of these we have already explained – stopping smoking. The second is not drinking alcohol. Alcohol is a toxic substance, and can damage our cells and our DNA, reducing our body's ability to fight against and prevent diseases such as lung cancer. Likewise, the diagram also recommends exercising. Exercising makes us fit and healthy – strengthening our chances of fighting off disease and infection.

Q18.

This image shows the carbon cycle, and the different stages that take place within this.

The carbon cycle begins with respiration. Plants and animals respire, sending carbon into the atmosphere in the form of carbon dioxide. Following this, the carbon dioxide is absorbed by producers such as plants, in order to make carbohydrates. This is a core part of the process of photosynthesis, and therefore the sun plays a big role in making this happen.

Next, animals feed on the plant that has absorbed the carbon dioxide. This passes the carbon compounds along the food chain. The carbon that the animals consume is then exhaled as carbon dioxide.

Following this, the animals die, and they decompose. When they decompose, the carbon in their bodies is then passed back into the atmosphere as carbon dioxide. The cycle then begins again. If the process of decomposition is blocked, for some reason, then the material left behind becomes fossil fuel.

Q19.

The infographic shows the process of a house being constructed, and then sold. The image shows all of the different stages.

The first stage is to get planning permission for the house. This is highly important, as you don't want to get halfway through building only to have to tear it down. After you've been approved for planning permission, you can start building the foundations for the house. The foundations provide a platform on which everything else can be built, and they are essential.

Next up, you need to construct the interior walls. The interior walls support the overall structure of the house, and are essentially the benchmark for how much space you would like in one particular room. After this, you can move onto the exterior walls – which provide additional support for the interior walls, and add a level of visual aesthetic from the outside looking in.

Following this, it's time to add the roof, which provides extra structural support, and then tile the roof – which helps to keep the natural elements away from your home!

Task 1: Answers

The penultimate stage is to decorate your home. The diagram emphasises the importance of good decoration – as this is a big part of what will persuade buyers to part with their money. Finally, it's time to sell the house!

Q20.

The infographic shows the various health benefits of lemon, and also some nutritional information. The list of benefits are shown via a series of pictures.

To start with, we have indigestion and constipation. Lemon is a useful way of treating this. Although it's highly acidic, small amounts of lemon mixed with water can alkalize the acid in your stomach. The infographic recommends mixing a tablespoon of lemon juice with a cup of water.

Following this, we have brain and nerve health. Lemon contains potassium, which improves concentration and memory. Potassium is fantastic for brain and nerve cells. The next item relates to dental care. This picture is warning you to be careful about drinking too much lemon, as it can be bad for your teeth – as it's very acidic. After this, we have heart health. Since lemon is high in vitamin C, which is good for your heart, naturally lemon reduces the risk of heart disease. Lemon is also a great way of managing respiratory diseases – since vitamin C reduces the production of molecules that can inflame the airways, as well as reducing the body's sensitivity to histamine – which makes allergies a lot easier to deal with.

Finally, the infographic informs us that lemon is a good way of dealing with rheumatism, since vitamin C helps to resolve joint cartilage problems.

Q21.

The infographic shows the process of ordering a shopping item, to be delivered to your home.

The first stage is the store. The infographic explains that goods are initially stocked at a warehouse, and then arrive at the store from there. Once they reach the store, they are separated into two categories: delivery (for customers ordering online) and front of house product (for customers coming into the store).

The next stage is the packing of the goods. When a customer orders a product online, the goods are packaged to be made ready for delivery. It's important that someone from the store runs a detailed check on the items, to make sure that everything is correct. Following this, the goods are loaded onto a van and sent out for delivery.

The delivery is made by a courier company, who have a set number of addresses to visit per day. Customers can generally track their goods using a tracking number, which will tell them how long it is before their product is delivered to them – between 9am and 5pm.

Once the customer receives their product, they are asked to leave an honest review. If they're unhappy with the product, then they have 14 days to return the item and receive a refund.

Q22.

The table in question shows statistics for the number of males and females who were convicted of certain crimes. There are 6 crimes listed in total, and the people listed are broken down into the following categories: Adult male, under 21 male, Adult female, under 21 Female, Convicted and Non-Convicted.

The first thing that should stand out when looking at this table is that the number of people convicted absolutely dwarfs the number of people who were not convicted. There are 3912 convictions, to just 465 non-convictions. In terms of gender there is quite a differential too. The only categories where male survey participants did not outnumber female was in theft and motoring offences, with all of other categories displaying a clear numerical sway towards men.

In terms of age, there was a clear numerical bias towards adults, who committed (regardless of conviction or non-conviction) 2544 crimes to 1833 crimes committed by people under the age of 21.

Q23.

The graph in question shows the musical preferences of people from the age of 10 and up. The music categories are drum and bass, country, rock, chart hits and pop.

When looking at this graph, the first thing we should be able to spot is that the most popular choice of music is chart hits. Chart hits scored highly in every single category, and was most popular with people aged 14-16. By far the least popular form of music was country, which did not score at all with people aged 10-13, nor in people aged 21+. In people aged 14-16 and 17-19, it did register, but scored poorly.

When it came to pop music, there was a clear trend, which was that pop music became less and less popular as people got older. In people aged 10-13, there were 12 people who said they liked pop. This decreased with people aged 14-16, with only 9 people saying they liked pop, then in people aged 17-19 this decreased sharply, with just 3 people saying they liked pop. Finally, in people aged 21+, there was just one person who said they liked pop.

Q24.

The graph shows the favourite animals of children between the ages of 3 and 19. Participants were given the choice of dog, cat, or hamster.

The first thing we should be able to spot when looking at this graph, is that dogs were by far the most popular choice. Dogs received 33 votes, compared to second place cats – which received 19 votes. In every single age group bar 7-11, dogs came out on top in popularity.

There was a clear pattern when it came to dogs, which became steadily more popular as people got older. There were 5 votes from people aged 3-6, then 7 votes from people aged 7-11, then 9 from people aged 12-15, and 12 from people aged 16-19.

None of the other two categories demonstrated a clear pattern, as cats went up one year, then down the next, before rising again, and the same with hamsters.

Q25.

The pie chart below shows the percentage of students in each GCSE subject at a local secondary school and the number of non-US students in the subject of Geography.

When looking at these pie charts, we should be able to spot that the most popular subject overall is Maths. Maths received 22% of the votes, in comparison to the next highest subject, which was Science with 17%. The lowest scoring subject was Geography – with just 8%.

Geography is the topic of the second pie chart, which shows the number of non-US students taking the subject. There were 118 students total in Geography, and 100 non-US students, meaning that non-US students made up approximately 85% of the total number.

The most common nationality in this chart was Australian, with 36 people in this category. There were 32 Europeans, and 21 Asians. The lowest scoring nationality in this chart was African, with just 11 people.

IELTS Academic
Writing: Task 2

As previously explained, Task 2 will consist of the following:

You'll be given a statement or question, and then asked to write 250 words discussing this. Your answer must be in essay format, using formal language. You will be marked on your ability to argue for/against in a persuasive fashion, using evidence, and examples based on your own personal experience too.

You'll have a total of 40 minutes to complete the assessment. Again, falling under the word count will result in you being penalised. The marks for task 2 are twice that of task 1, meaning that failure to complete this exercise will greatly harm your chances of scoring highly.

During this assessment, the main elements that are being tested are in relation to the fluency of your writing and vocabulary. You are also being tested on how well your response is structured, how well it uses persuasive language, and how well it cites information and ideas. Basically, you need to put together a coherent and logical response, paying attention to grammar, spelling and punctuation, whilst addressing the main statement from the question.

Let's start out by looking at an example:

> 'Technology is harmful to human interaction.'

How To Answer This

If you've ever written an essay, you might be familiar with the general structure of how to approach a question like this. However, in the IELTS Task 2, you have a limited amount of time and words. This means that you need to be short and concise with what you are saying. In a normal essay, you might take the time to acknowledge counter arguments and alternative points of view. Since you've only got 250 words (or slightly more) for this task, it's advised that you focus on just arguing for or against the topic. While you can of course make passing reference to other points of view, keep these brief, and stay focused on the argument that you are trying to make. Remember that you are trying to be persuasive, and highlight that your point of view is the correct one.

There are two structural approaches that you can take to an essay, and in this book we have provided you with examples of both. These are as follows:

Plain and simple.

This aptly named way of writing an essay is exactly what it sounds like. You start out by responding to the statement. For example:

'I agree with the statement. I believe that technology is harmful to human interaction. The reasons that I believe this are as follows.'

Here you have clearly laid out your viewpoint, and now you can move onto the main body of the essay. The difference between this and a longer essay is again, the time and number of words that you have. Whilst in a longer essay you might start out by talking about different forms of technology, definitions of the word harmful, and other such speculation – in the IELTS essay it's better to get straight to the point. 250 words is not a huge amount.

Following this, the main body of the essay should be pretty simple. Write one to three reasons why you agree (or disagree) with the statement. For example:

'Firstly, I believe that...'

'Secondly, we must consider that...'

'Thirdly, it is important to recognise that...'

Finally, we have the conclusion. In your conclusion, you should basically summarise the main point of the essay. For example:

'In conclusion, I feel that technology is harmful to human interaction, because it has a sustained impact on the way we behave face-to-face.'

Freeform

Freeform essays are a bit trickier than the above, and should only be attempted if you feel really confident in your essay writing skills. Freeform does not use the 'structure' of the above method. While it focuses on roughly the same things, freeform essays are more similar to the method that you might use to write a longer piece of work. Below we've included an example, so that you can see how different this might look:

'Discuss the value of tonal consistency in fiction'

Sample Response

In recent years, a popular criticism of works of fiction is a lack of tonal consistency. By this, it is meant that a piece of fiction plays too fast-and-loose with its tone, creating moments which can be considered 'jarring' and critically undesirable.

For example, if an episode of a television show cuts from a scene of brutal violence to one of joking and laughter, an audience member might experience a feeling of tonal 'whiplash'. What emotion are they supposed to be feeling: the horror of the violence in scene one, or the joy of scene two? By moving so quickly from one extreme to another, some members of the audience might not be sure about how to frame a certain scene, resulting in a less satisfying experience. This criticism can be found across modern fiction, from superhero movies to popular television shows.

However, is tonal inconsistency a real problem in fiction, or is it just a trendy new way of examining it? Despite many big-budget films being criticised for having an inconsistent tone, much of these releases still perform incredibly well at the box office. Perhaps this is just a problem that critics have with modern storytelling, whilst audiences don't mind it so much.

It may also be the case that the problem is culturally relative. Other forms of foreign media, such as Japanese anime, are more willing to shift between extreme tones. In some anime television shows, the tone may turn from one of light-hearted happiness and relief to one of crushing fear or disgust – sometimes in the space of a single scene.

Some have argued that these sudden changes in tone are more true-to-life than tonally consistent pieces of work. After all, each day in a person's life doesn't have a single mood; our lives are dotted with constant highs and lows. Similarly, the tone of our lives can go from happiness to horror in an instant. Therefore, we shouldn't be afraid to reflect this in our fiction.

Hopefully you should be able to see that the above response uses a very different structure to the type of response we showed before. Instead of using simple terms, 'Here is the beginning, 'Here is part 1' 'Here is part 2', 'Here is my conclusion' this essay simply talks about the subject, in a way that ends naturally rather than being structured into recognisable sub-sections.

Whichever you way you choose to write your essay, you should use what is comfortable for you, and there is no right or wrong way to respond – just as long as your response is persuasive, logical and consistent. You also need to pay attention to grammar, because you will be marked down for this if you make mistakes.

Now, let's look at some sample questions!

Task 2: Practice Questions

Q1. *'Humans should not be held responsible for the care of the environment, or what happens to the planet.'*

Discuss whether you agree or disagree with the above statement.

Q2. *'Creative Writing cannot be taught at university. There are too many factors that muddy the water of 'teaching' writing, for it to be considered legitimate teaching.'*

Discuss the validity of the above statement.

Q3. 'Music should be free for everyone. The government should legalise the practice of downloading music from websites such as YouTube.'

Discuss the validity of the above statement.

Q4. *Evaluate the pros and cons of self-publishing vs traditional publishing.*

Q5. *'Fake news is not harmful, and its negative effect on society is greatly exaggerated.'*

Discuss the merits of the above statement.

Task 2: Practice Questions

Q6. *'War is a terrible course of action, and only leads to negative consequences.'*

Discuss the merits of the above statement.

Q7. *'Darts is unfairly maligned, and should be considered an Olympic Sport.'*

Discuss the merits of the above statement.

Q8. *'Animals should not be given the same rights as humans, because they are not sentient.'*

Discuss the merits of the above statement.

Q9. *'We have no moral obligation to people we've never met.'*

Discuss the value of the above statement.

Q10. 'Social networking is by nature a dangerous phenomenon, and puts people's data at risk.'

Discuss the value of the above statement.

Q11. *Discuss whether violence can ever be justified.*

Q12. *'Authors don't need to make their fictional worlds internally consistent. They should focus on entertaining the reader.'*

Evaluate the merits of the above statement.

Q13. *'There is no definitive answer to what represents 'good' or 'bad' art. Therefore, we can only form opinions on artwork, not facts.'*

Discuss the veracity of the above statement.

Q14. *'When making decisions, there is far more value in thinking rationally than there is in thinking emotionally.'*

Discuss whether you agree or disagree with the above statement.

Q15. *'Ethical veganism is not truly ethical. There are too many holes in this belief for it to be considered legitimate.'*

Discuss whether you agree with the above statement.

Q16. 'Space exploration is dangerous, and human beings should avoid venturing into the unknown. By doing so, we are risking our safety as a species.'

Discuss whether you agree with the above statement.

Q17. 'Human beings cannot be blamed for global warming. Our impact on the environment is a drop in the ocean compared to the natural processes of the world.'

Discuss your view on the above statement.

Q18. *'Gun control in the United States is wholly unnecessary, and puts more lives at risk. People should be able to carry a weapon in public, as long as it's done in a discrete manner.'*

Discuss the merits of the above statement.

Q19. *'Same sex marriage is a great concept, and something that should be welcomed by all countries.'*

Discuss whether you agree or disagree with the above statement.

Q20. *'Combat sports should be treated the same way as any other sport, and should be taught in schools.'*

Discuss your view on the above statement.

Q21. *'PE should not be compulsory. It is abhorrent and unfair to force children at school to exercise.'*

Discuss your views on the above statement.

Q22. 'It doesn't matter if certain species become extinct. There are plenty of other species well equipped to step into the gap.'

Discuss the above statement.

Q23. *"Monarchy is an outdated and unnecessary concept, and should be abolished with immediate effect.'*

Discuss the validity of the above statement.

Q24. *'Euthanasia should be legalised. Every person should have the right to decide if, when, and how they want to end their life.'*

Discuss your views on the above statement.

Q25. *'Patriotism is illogical, and creates problems for society.'*

Discuss the validity of the above statement.

Task 2: Answers

Q1.

On a fundamental level, I disagree with this statement. I strongly believe that human beings do have a responsibility to look after the world we live in, and that we have a duty of care to the planet.

Firstly, we cannot look beyond the fact that human beings have had a huge (and arguably negative) impact on the planet. Through burning fossil fuels, and deforestation, we have greatly contributed to global warming – the gradual rise in the Earth's temperature. Therefore, it goes without saying that human beings should take better responsibility for their actions and attempt steps to amend their behaviour.

Secondly, although human beings are a law unto themselves, we must take responsibility and care for the other species and life on our planet. We are destroying the earth, without due thought for these species and their way of life. This is a selfish attitude. As human beings, we have been blessed with extraordinary intelligence, far surpassing that of other species. With this intelligence comes responsibility, and we must use this to look after the planet. Instead, we are using this intelligence to exploit the planet's natural resources.

Thirdly, I believe that human beings should be grateful for the planet we have been given. Earth is a thing of beauty, and our lack of care as an overall species is astounding. As human beings, we are taught to be respectful towards others and their possessions. However, as a species we are showing a profound lack of respect for Earth, and the gifts that it brings us.

In conclusion, I believe that the speaker is wrong. Human beings are duty-bound to care for the environment and take responsibility for fixing our own environmental mistakes.

Q2.

I largely agree with the above statement that Creative Writing cannot be taught. However, I do not feel that this is all-encompassing, and there are some benefits to the teaching of Creative Writing.

The reasons I agree with the statement are as follows:

Firstly, there are the teachers themselves. Although it's entirely possible for a writer to approach different kinds of fiction in a different way, the majority of writers lean towards one style of fiction. We all have our own style of writing, that we also enjoy reading. When giving advice or critiquing other writer's work, we naturally lean towards an opinion that corresponds with our own. This is dangerous when it comes to new and aspiring writers, who are still searching for a way to define their own style.

Secondly, there is the marking system itself. Along with the fact that the markers are naturally biased, how it is that writing can be assigned a marked score? Can you really grade a piece of writing from 1-100? Written fiction is not the same as an essay, it is subjective, and to assign a score from 1-100 or even a grade, seems benign. The whole point of a creative writing degree is that you should improve as a writer, not what mark you get at the end of it.

Despite the above, I still believe there are certain benefits to the teaching of Creative Writing. Although you cannot 'teach' someone to write a book, you can help them with smaller aspects – such as giving them ideas on how to improve their written speech, their characterisation and their plot. As the saying goes, 'two heads are better than one'.

In conclusion, I believe that although Creative Writing cannot be taught in a way that justifies it as a degree, there are some benefits to the teaching of this subject. Namely, that there is nothing wrong with providing others with helpful advice, just as long as we recognise the limitations of this advice.

Q3.

I strongly disagree with the above statement. I do not believe that music should be given this treatment, and I feel that the practice of downloading music from websites (without paying) is extremely harmful.

First of all, we must consider the impact that such behaviour has on the artists. By illegally downloading their music from the internet, you are bypassing the option to pay them for their services. Thus, you are acquiring a completely free product, with no benefit for the person who provided it to you. You would not walk into a shop and simply take something from the shelves, so why would it be considered acceptable to steal music? Music artists are people, just like anyone else, trying to make a living. By stealing their music you are effectively putting your hand in their pocket.

Secondly, as mentioned, this practice is harmful. It's harmful not only to the artists, but to the music industry as a whole. The bottom line is this: the money that you pay for music goes towards more music. Therefore, on a basic level, by paying for music you are essentially putting an investment towards more content that you enjoy. If everyone took their music from the internet instead of paying for it, then both the quality of music as a whole and the number of songs released/artists would dwindle – which would ultimately harm everyone.

In conclusion, I believe that the practice of taking music from the internet is fundamentally negative and is not something the government should consider legalising. Music thieves are harmful to the industry, and to artists as a whole.

Q4.

I believe that self-publishing has a number of pros compared to traditional publishing, albeit there are a few cons too.

Firstly, the biggest advantage of self-publishing is that the author gets to maintain a significant portion of the control over their own work. They are given the freedom to choose the book cover, the title, and even what goes into the content. When you sign with a traditional publisher, there is a good chance that you will lose the rights to decide these things – as part of the contract means that the publishing house can make decisions on such elements. This is significant for authors, who are likely to feel a degree of emotional attachment to their work.

Secondly, there are the royalties. Self-publishing has a far better royalty rate for authors than traditional publishing. In fact, excluding the cost of printing and delivery, self-published authors get to keep one hundred percent of the profits from their book. This is not the case with traditional publishing, where authors receive at most thirty percent of the royalties, depending on what contract they are given.

Despite these two benefits, there are some drawbacks to self-publishing. The most significant of these is the marketing element. Whilst you can do a stellar job of marketing your own book, the bottom line is that traditional publishing houses have numerous contacts within the industry, and garner more respect from those outlets (such as advertising agencies and newspapers) which are best placed to advertise the book to a wider audience.

In conclusion, I feel that self-publishing has a number of benefits, which largely outweigh the negatives. For this reason, I believe that self-publishing is a highly worthwhile venture.

Q5.

Fake news can be defined as 'a type of journalism which focuses on deliberate dissemination of misinformation and hoaxes – usually to serve an agenda.' I disagree with the statement maker. I believe that fake news is harmful to society. The primary reason for this is as follows:

Our modern social and technological landscape makes fake news a bigger threat than ever. The most important angle we need to examine is how technology and society have merged over the past ten years or so. The dramatic rise of social media, forums, online video gaming, and other platforms have led the internet to become a fragmented place, split into countless communities. Those who wish to spread fake news can infect these fragmented communities. Without a unified society to watch over each other's shoulders, hoax-spreaders can get to work on manipulating different subsets of internet society into essentially working for them.

Whether these subcultures are inherently political or not is irrelevant: all it takes is an opportunistic group of propagandists to convince a subset of internet society that a political event matters to them. From there, the community can be convinced to spread false information on the propagandists' behalf. The very nature of modern social media means that it's incredibly easy to spread false information. All it takes is a credible-looking thumbnail image and hyperlink, combined with a sensationalist headline, for misinformation to swell across the internet. Fake news can bound its way across the internet, and since many people don't think to corroborate the information, what was once nonsense is now accepted as fact.

In conclusion, I believe that fake news, and spreading misinformation, is extremely harmful. As a society, we should seek the truth, and strongly discourage the spread of lies and falsities.

Q6.

Whilst the above statement contains some level of truth, I do not completely agree with it. It's undeniable that war is a terrible thing, and that most people would argue that the world would be better off without conflict, but I do not believe that we can completely discredit war as pure evil.

Firstly, there are numerous technological and medical advancements which would never have been made were it not for warfare. Penicillin likely wouldn't have been mass-produced were it not for the Second World War, which would mean that the modern world would lack vital antibiotics. Likewise, the x-ray machine was developed because of its usefulness in diagnosing wounds during the First World War. Were it not for the Second World War and the allied powers' bombings of Hiroshima and Nagasaki, we might not have developed nuclear energy. If necessity is the mother of invention, then war is the greatest inventor of them all.

Technological advancements aside, war and conflict can lead to social and political progress. Organisations such as the United Nations were established as a result of the Second World War, ushering in an era of globalised economies and political structures. The Second World War also ended in the destruction of the Nazis as a global power. This is surely a cause for celebration.

So, it's clear that war is far from a good thing overall. However, to completely dismiss the positive outcomes of war, and how much our modern world has benefitted from it, would be incredibly naïve.

Q7.

I am in full agreement with the above statement, and I believe that there is no defining quality which means that darts should not be considered for the Olympics. The reasons I believe this as are follows:

Firstly, it is arguable that disregarding darts comes down to pure snobbery. It's incorrectly assumed that some sports are better than others because of how much running or physical exercise their participants incur. Can we use this to objectively rank the sports? Is football more of a sport than volleyball because it requires more energy? Must we use physical exertion as a means of defining what is a sport, and what isn't?

Secondly, like art, there's no clear way of defining what constitutes a sport and what doesn't. This leaves us with the issue of deciding what counts as a sport and what doesn't. In turn, what should constitute an Olympic sport? Without any objective guidance, we must rely on completely subjective standards for defining sports at an Olympic level. The closest to an objective metric that we have is demand. The more demand there is for a sport to be shown at the Olympics, the more it should be considered. If people want darts to appear at the Olympics, they need to make their voices heard.

Ultimately, darts should be made into an Olympic sport because it would bring an element of realism to the games. The sports at the Olympics are for the elite, such as gymnastics. What the Olympics need are more sports that the everyday person can enjoy. By refusing to show a range of sports that meet various types of people's tastes, the Olympics exposes itself as an event purely for the rich and affluent.

Q8.

The above statement is very complex, and raises a number of issues. Whilst I disagree with the tone of the speaker, as I do believe that animals have rights, the issue of sentience is decidedly more murky.

When discussing the moral status of animals, the first topic of debate revolves around sentience. The general belief among many ethicists is that, so long as something is sentient, then it ought to have some degree of rights. Sentience usually encompasses the following three main notions: the capacity to feel pleasure and pain, have perceptions, or to have subjective experiences about the world. What you might notice is that these three qualities are rather distinct from one another.

While these three notions are all somewhat different, what we do know is that most humans possess all three. Human beings can experience pleasure and pain, are capable of interpreting sensory data, and also have subjective experiences about the world. Therefore, humans are sentient on all three counts. In turn, this means that they should have rights.

One of the most significant arguments against animals being sentient, and therefore not deserving rights, comes from a position of scepticism. As a human being, I can verify that I experience pleasure and pain, can interpret sense data, and have subjective experiences. Hence, I can assume that most, if not all, other human beings are also sentient. In the case of non-human animals, no such justification is warranted. I am not a cat, dog, horse, or mayfly, and therefore I cannot verify that my experiences of sentience are enjoyed by them as well. Since we cannot prove that animals possess any of these qualities, then we must assume that they do not.

Q9.

I fundamentally disagree with the above statement. I believe that not having met someone should not be used as an excuse for displaying a lack of morals towards that person, and that as members of the human race we have a duty of care and responsibility for each other. The primary reason I believe this is as follows:

Let's take an example of someone we will never meet, but certainly have a moral connection with. Most of our clothes in the Western world are produced in South and South-East Asia. The people who work in the factories that manufacture these garments are often paid quite poorly, at least by Western standards. This is one of the ways in which retailers can sell clothes for much cheaper. So, when we save money by buying cheap clothes, this is as a result of potentially exploited workers in foreign countries. Essentially, the cheap pair of jeans you bought only exist because someone in a faraway land is underpaid. We benefit from their exploitation, but do we have a moral obligation to them? I'll never meet the people in Sri Lanka who stitched my shirt together, so why should I care about them? Based on this argument I should save my "moral energy" for those closer to me, and leave the worrying about disadvantaged people overseas to their own friends and family.

The principal issue with this mode of thinking is that it doesn't demonstrate a clear cut-off point for where you should stop caring about people. I should care about myself, my immediate family, friends, and extended family – this is fairly uncontroversial. However, what about my family's friends, or my friends' families? Are they outside of my apathy wall? The answer is no.

In conclusion, I believe that the statement in question is flawed, and does not take into account our responsibility as human beings, nor does it address the complex social webs built into relationship concepts such as family, or even distant family.

Q10.

I largely agree with the statement above. However, whilst I believe that there are risks associated with social media, this does not make it dangerous by nature. It is simply used in this way, by people exploiting the tool for information. Let's look at exactly why this is the case:

Firstly, there is the fact that information posted on these sites is likely to come back and haunt a person in the future. Just think of a social networking site as a type of "global database". You are posting information, facts about yourself, images etc, into your very own "database", acting as a log of your personal behaviour for others to view. This is a great concern for many parents whereby they feel obliged to check how secure their child is whilst they're online.

An example of the impact of social networking occurred in America, whereby students were faced with court charges for underage drinking, a situation that had it not been shared on their social networking profiles, would never have been known otherwise. The students in question were unaware of the impact of their behaviour of underage drinking and posting the evidence online.

Social media sites are also becoming an increasing concern in terms of bullying, grooming and abuse. With a small minority of users utilising the security system to its fullest, profiles are subsequently left open to everyone. A profile can be used to track down someone, find out what someone is up to, stalk an individual, and become somewhat obsessive over the lives of other people.

In conclusion, I do believe that social media sites can be seen as dangerous – for all of the reasons listed above, but I do not think that social media is dangerous by nature, given that it was created in part to connect people from all over the world in a positive manner.

Q11.

Many people believe that violence, conflict, and evil are intertwined. Violence is a central part of ethics, with violent behaviour generally being considered immoral. While this is mostly true, it's also a slight simplification of how the world really works.

Ideally, all conflict in the world would be avoided altogether, and we should continue to strive for a conflict-free world. Until then, however, there will always be those who use violence as a means of disorder. Sometimes, the only way to prevent this violence is through more violence: albeit more targeted, skilful, and measured. The only way to destroy a terror cell might be to kill its leader, or at least use violent means of capturing them.

However, there are a few issues with this line of reasoning. Firstly, is it possible to create a peaceful world through conflict? Wars have been fought for righteous, "peace-making" causes for hundreds (if not thousands) of years, yet we are still faced with more violence and conflict. Using violence as a means of creating less violence is clearly ineffective, and therefore it shouldn't be justified on utilitarian grounds. Moreover, there's no reason to believe that it is only guilty people who have been killed in these peace-keeping efforts.

We should also consider who we are giving the power to decide who lives and who dies to. Surely the only person who would desire such a responsibility is someone who is bloodthirsty, and therefore they are more likely to permit violence towards innocents. However, someone who is more measured is less likely to want the position. This means that the people who are employed to make these decisions are always the worst people to do so. Therefore, violence is not justified.

Q12.

To a large extent, I agree with the above statement. I strongly feel that authors should be given leeway when it comes to creating their own fictional world. However, there are still a few rules which they should abide by. The reasons I believe this are as follows:

Firstly, if the goal of a fictional world is to be entertaining, then the author should use every method at their disposal to do so. In some cases, this might involve breaking internal consistency in order to tell a more meaningful story. For example, a lack of consistency between scenes might demonstrate a communication breakdown between two or more characters, or even be used as a metaphor for one's own internal inconsistency. So, a lack of consistency within a fictional world can create deeper meaning, which might give certain audiences greater enjoyment.

Secondly, storytelling is ultimately just what the name suggests: telling a story. In recent years, fiction has moved from individual stories to expanded universes, which has invited the need for every event, character, and motive to click into place as though their stories are world history. The more we focus on these expanded universes, the less we lose the core of what made storytelling so unique: its fundamental difference from the real world in that it doesn't need to be internally coherent.

However, a level of verisimilitude is essential for a piece of fiction to be taken seriously. The more believable a fictional world is, the easier it will be for the audience to get invested in it. For example, if the power of a weapon is described in one scene as being able to destroy whole planets, but later is shown to be far weaker, this could break the immersion for the audience.

In conclusion, I agree that authors should not be bound by rules over the veracity or consistency over their fictional worlds. However, a good author will exercise restraint, and understand where inconsistency helps and where it doesn't.

Q13.

The notion of 'what is good' is a very popular topic amongst philosophers. By this, they mean not to discuss which things constitute as being "good", but rather which standards can objectively determine "good" works from others. While some search for a means of demonstrating how a piece of art can be objectively "good", others have given up entirely on such a venture, instead stating that there is no objective "good". Therefore, what is deemed to be of high quality or low quality is completely subjective: there is no fact of the matter about the quality of artworks, only opinions.

The Scottish philosopher David Hume highlighted the issue of taste, art, and subjectivity in Of the Standard of Taste. While not the first to tackle this issue, Hume opened debate by breaking down the argument surrounding art, objectivity, and taste by highlighting the core issue. In this essay, Hume identified two sets of data which seem to contradict one another. On the one hand, people often say "each to their own" when it comes to matters of taste, such as their favourite piece of music or painting. However, many also appear to hold the view that some artworks are fundamentally better than others. Only one of these statements can be true.

When presented with these two claims, we have a choice of two options. The first is to align with the first datum and argue that there is no objective truth when it comes to art and taste – "good" is left to the beholder. Following this, we are left with sheer subjectivity when it comes to art.

The position of total subjectivity may be tempting when discussing art. After all, who am I to say that my artistic preferences are objectively better than yours? If we have no means of independently demonstrating which piece of art is better than another, then the default position must be that there is no objective truth in terms of art and taste.

Q14.

The debate between emotional and rational thinking, or 'head vs heart' is a very commonly discussed matter. In my opinion, there is a lot of value in thinking emotionally, as opposed to rationally. Therefore, I disagree with this statement. The reasons for this are as follows:

Firstly, it seems to me that there is something of an obsession with rejecting one's feelings and opting for a purely logical approach when approaching ethical or practical issues. Perhaps it is a result of renaissance thinking: that each and every one of us is a rational being capable of 'thinking through' all of our problems. Remaining composed is valued above listening to one's own emotions, but where have our ethical theories got us? Whether it's utilitarianism, deontology, or divine command theory, all of our rational means of making ethical decisions are inherently flawed. Emotion, however, remains pure and infallible.

Secondly, I believe that emotion is a more powerful tool than reason when making ethical decisions because it is more natural. Reason is useful for giving us information about the world, but it is ultimately abstract: no matter how many facts and figures you present to me about a moral crisis, you will not necessarily provoke a specific ethical response. Information and reasoning systems such as utilitarianism are more focused with cold, hard facts than they are the reality of a situation. In contrast, our emotions are a fundamental part of what it means to be human, and they give us greater insight when making a moral decision.

In summary, I believe that emotion is a more natural and therefore appropriate way to approach decisions. As human beings, we should act on how we feel inwardly, rather than expecting our brains to think logically about every last situation. This is fundamentally impossible, given the way that humans experience emotion and feelings.

Q15.

Ethical veganism refers to veganism for animal rights purposes. This definition is used to distinguish it from environmental veganism, and dietary veganism. There are also those who are vegan for purely cultural reasons, with ethical and environmental concerns possessing no influence on their lifestyle choice. However, is ethical veganism really so ethical? While refusing to consume products which are associated with animal cruelty is certainly an ethical decision, it carries implications which aren't so moral. For these reasons, ethical veganism isn't as morally valuable as a vegan would have you believe.

For example, a vegan diet in the modern Western world consists of a range of products, many of which aren't seasonal. Thanks to globalisation, the entire world is a web of train, plane, and boat links, allowing for people to get all kinds of fruit, vegetables, and other products that are suitable for vegans to eat. While this means that vegans can enjoy a varied and balanced diet, it also has negative impacts on the world. The carbon footprint caused by importing from across the globe must be disastrous. So, an ethical vegan directly contributes to climate change.

The second major moral dilemma worth discussing is as much an issue with capitalism in general as it is ethical veganism specifically. In order to meet the demands of a vegan population, a significant number of farmhands are necessary to work the land. To keep the costs of these products as low as possible, these labourers are often paid poorly and work under uncomfortable conditions. In some cases, it has been suggested that the labourers are mostly migrant workers who are being exploited for the gain of wealthy people in Western countries. So, this means that the ethical vegan implicitly endorses the exploitation of human beings, so long as animals are safe and looked after.

In conclusion, I agree with the statement. I do not believe that ethical veganism is truly ethical, and that there are a number of factors, including human exploitation, which count against this view.

Q16.

I largely disagree with the above statement. In my opinion, space exploration is vital to our progression as a species, and human beings should seek to test the limits of our knowledge. The reasons I believe this are as follows:

Firstly, as human beings, we have conquered the world. Over the decades, our combined and cumulative efforts have allowed us to map the entire planet. We know so much about the world we live in, and are truly masters of our environments. It's about time we found a new frontier, and given our domination of the lands, it's time that we take to the stars for new adventures and opportunities. The thing that makes us human is our primal urge for discovery. Therefore, we have no choice but to invest in space exploration and travel further than we ever have before.

Space exploration is more than just a frivolous venture into the unknown: it's an investment in our future. Space exploration requires a range of workers from all kinds of fields and classes. Physicists and engineers will be vital for design, whilst logistics and manual labourers will be needed in order to construct our chariots of the heavens. Moreover, exploration in the future might give us access to resources that we sadly lack on our own planet. New energy solutions on other worlds might be our saving grace as our own climate and environments fall apart. Space exploration isn't just a pipe-dream, it's a definitive way to create jobs and save our species, with all the wanderlust that the movies demonstrate as well.

In conclusion, I see space exploration as a way for human beings to access new resources, broaden our minds and understand the universe around us. For these reasons, I believe that it is vital that we continue to explore.

Q17.

I believe that the above statement is fundamentally incorrect, and that human beings have had a massive impact on the planet. In many cases, our actions are reckless and have caused irreparable damage to the Earth.

Burning fossil fuels is a clear example of how, over the past 15 decades, human beings have impacted the environment. The world has become more industrialised and changed the balance of the carbon cycle. Burning fossil fuels such as oil, gas and coal converts carbon into carbon dioxide, and unless it is captured, the carbon dioxide is released into the atmosphere. This climate change is characterised by higher than average global temperatures and the increased sea levels.

Forests have a huge role to play in fighting climate change. Forests can be used to absorb and store carbon in their soil and trees.

Yet, we continue to cut these forests down with no hindsight of the consequences that follow. Why? Why do we continue these actions if we know what the outcome and consequences are going to be?

If these forests are frequently being cut down, then all the stored emissions from the trees, will be released into the atmosphere. Up to one fifth of greenhouse gas emissions comes from deforestation and forest degradation, which indicates the scale of the issue and the impact it causes in terms of global warming.

Some people consider global warming as "natural", yet it is apparent that we, as the contributing factors to climate change, need to change our behaviour. Science tells us that although the Earth's climate has always changed, our actions in the way we have treated our planet remain the most damaging.

Q18.

I do not agree with the speaker of this statement. I feel that carrying concealed weapons comes with its own set of problems, and that gun control would almost certainly save more lives.

One of the most commonly cited reasons for carrying weapons, from progun activists, is that people have a right to defend themselves against the government. These people are, quite frankly, deluded. In the unlikely event that the government did decide to turn against its citizens, a handgun would not be much use. The government has tanks, drones, planes and bombs at its disposal. Unless these people would change the law to allow all citizens access to rocket launchers and other heavy weaponry, they will have to reconcile themselves with the uncomfortable truth that a physical resistance against the US Government would be virtually impossible.

Equally as ridiculous is the argument that gun control laws violate the second amendment. The second amendment states, 'a well-regulated militia being necessary to the security of the Free State, the right of the people to keep and bear Arms shall not be infringed'. This is all well and good, if you ignore the power of the US military. Is it really necessary to have a citizen based military, just to ensure American sovereignty? The US military is the strongest armed force in the world.

The majority of studies have shown that gun laws reduce violence. Some people argue that it's not guns that kill people, it is people that kill people. That might be true, but people with guns kill more people than they would if they didn't have guns. For this reason, I believe that the statement is simply incorrect.

Q19.

I absolutely agree with the above statement. I believe that there are a huge number of reasons to welcome same sex marriage, and it is hard to believe that certain sections of society have not yet evolved or adapted to this accepting and welcoming way of thinking.

Using the UK as an example, within the first three months of same-sex marriage becoming legalised in the UK, over 1,400 ceremonies were conducted for gay marriages. This has led to powerful signals that promote gay marriage as loving and committed, and shows British culture as respecting and tolerant. As a child, we are continuously told to pursue our dreams, and to be "ourselves". If a person then grows up choosing to follow the path of being gay, they should have the right to do so. They should not be prone to disgruntled glances and constant remarks behind their backs. Gay people should not feel as though they are 10 years old and back on the playground, defending themselves. They should be able to feel mature and accepted for the person they have chosen to be, and indulge in a lifestyle that doesn't affect anyone but themselves.

Same sex marraiges are correlated with lower divorce rates, provide stability in association to marital status, and bring financial gain to its government. So, why do they continue to be ridiculed?

A person should be with the person they wish to spend their life with, the same way a person chooses to have a baby, or have cosmetic surgery, or chooses to donate blood. A person's choice, is a person's life. It is up to them to choose how they define themselves.

Q20.

I do not agree with the above statement. Whilst I do not believe that combat sports should be marginalised, there would be clear issues with teaching such sports in schools.

We are taught as a child that violence is bad, and that we shouldn't use aggressive behaviour as a means of resolution. Combatants in combat sports are trained in using techniques to subdue their opponent. Thus, we must ask ourselves an important question: how ethical are such sports? Although there is some value in teaching young people how to defend themselves, we should not be encouraging aggression. Combat should not be deemed 'normal'.

It can also be argued that less aggressive sports that contain reckless behaviour such as football and rugby sometimes result in injury. Yet, these teams and people do not win the game by implementing any force or aggression; they win because of the number of goals or points they score. Whereas, combat sports intentionally set out to fight and defeat an opponent. In these sports, you can only win by causing enough conflict for a combatant to be unable to continue.

It can also be argued that children who are constantly exposed to violent and aggressive behaviour will display negative long-term developmental effects, skewed social behaviour and ideas about what is right and wrong. If a child is taught to fight in order to protect themselves from losing, how can they recognise when it is safe to do this?

Teaching combat sport in schools risks children being unable to distinguish between situations that require certain types of behaviour i.e. acceptable behaviour in different types of sports, and every day behaviour at home, in the classroom, on the playground etc. The risk is not worth the reward, and therefore I do not believe combat sports should be taught in schools.

Q21.

One popular topic of debate amongst academics is on whether Physical Education, that is at least the physical side of PE, should be compulsory for GCSE students. Current educational requirements state that students under the age of 17 must take part in a minimum number of hours of physical activity per week at school. The question is – is this fair? Should students be forced to exercise?

In my opinion, yes they should. There is a bevy of scientific evidence to support the fact that a lack of early exercise leads to problems such as obesity and diabetes, and therefore it's imperative that schools play an active role in ironing this out. The problem is not with PE itself, but with the way PE lessons are run, and the type of exercise that children are being made to perform. Can you really blame children for not wanting to run 1500m around a track, in below 0 temperatures? Coupled with the fact that most school PE uniforms consist of tiny shorts and a thin top, it's no surprise that children are reluctant.

Furthermore, Britain has a growing obesity problem, and it's up to schools to stamp this out early. Statistics show that if we don't take a stand now, obesity rates will roar by 2030. In the USA alone, it is estimated that at least half the population will be obese unless something is done. Britain faces a similar issue. Doctors have highlighted a 30% increase in the rise of obesity in England alone, within the last 20 years. If we don't act soon; it will be far too late.

Q22.

I believe that the above statement is fundamentally wrong on a number of levels. Any species becoming extinct will have a major impact. The reasons for this are as follows:

Firstly, we must look at the impact that the extinction of a species has on the ecosystem as a whole. If we eliminate one species from the food chain, this can have unpredictable and dangerous consequences. For example, organism A gets eaten by organism B, and organism B gets eaten by organism C. If you remove organism A from the food chain, then organism B will lose its source of food and could die out, which in turn will have the same impact on organism C. On the other hand, organism B could start eating elsewhere, having an impact on another food chain. Thus, you can see how the extinction of a species has extremely far reaching consequences for many other species too.

Secondly, we must look at this question from a moral perspective. It isn't a case of whether it 'matters', it is a case of right and wrong. We would have a fundamental issue with someone who claimed that the human race needed to be made extinct, therefore we should take the same attitude towards other organisms on our planet.

Furthermore, the extinction of a certain species would have a significant impact on a number of people too. All around the world, there are specific conservation groups set up for every single animal. Whether it's tigers, bears, lions or antelopes, there are trusts and charities set up to fund their survival. The extinction of a certain species would lead to widespread outrage.

The bottom line is that the extinction of any species would have far reaching effects. The natural ecosystem is a delicate chain, which has been crafted over hundreds of thousands of years of predator-prey relations. To throw a curveball such as extinction into the mix, would be devastating. Therefore, it is safe to say that the extinction of a species would matter a great deal.

Q23.

I disagree with the above statement. On a personal level, I feel that the UK monarchy plays a very important role in our lives. The reasons I believe this are as follows:

Firstly, I believe that the monarchy acts an essential representation of our heritage and culture. The Queen is a living reminder of everything has been, and what has shaped the country. She provides an extremely powerful focus for loyalty and patriotism, and serves as a source of strength, endurance and tradition during difficult times. From a moral standpoint, this is hugely important for the citizens of the United Kingdom.

Secondly, I would argue that having a monarch historically causes far fewer problems than having an elected government. There is no political gridlock or conflict when a monarch is in charge of the nation, and reduces tension amongst the public who voted for 'the other party'. A monarch is democratically accountable, and holds real power, rather than power that must be agreed or conferred by several other groups of people.

Thirdly, you could argue that the monarchy of the United Kingdom actually brings in far more money than it takes. The monarchy represent the UK all over the globe, and The Queen is known to have shaken more hands than any other person in history. This brings in essential tourist revenue, as millions of people everyday visit sites that are associated with royalty.

In conclusion, whether it's worldwide or just in the United Kingdom, I believe that it's incorrect to label monarchy as 'unnecessary'. Monarchs play an important role in national affairs, and provide a fantastic morale boost for the citizens of their country.

Q24.

I agree with the above statement. I strongly feel that euthanasia is something that should be legalised. The reasons I believe this are as follows:

Firstly, I believe that people should have a choice. As per human rights, they should be able to choose when to end their life. Just as they have a right to live, they have a right to die. Provided this does not bring physical harm to any other citizen, it is unfair to force people to live if they do not want to. People should be given autonomy and control over their own future.

Secondly, I think it is worth considering that there are worse things than death. For many people, living a life where an illness is slowly destroying their mind, their organs are failing or they are hooked up to artificial support; is equal to a second-rate existence. Many of these people would rather die than live like this, in unimaginable pain and suffering. It could be argued that it is far more humane to allow people in this state to choose their own death, than force them to go through even more pain and suffering, all the while knowing that they will die anyway.

Thirdly, you could argue that legalised euthanasia would improve the economy. By giving sufferers the choice to end their own lives, you would reduce the cost and time spent by the NHS who are ultimately trying to comfort and support patients who don't actually want to be alive. Very often, the medication that is assigned to deal with these issues or prolong a sufferer's life, will leave them in a state of delirium or even worse pain than before. End of life medication is not designed to save people. It is extremely expensive and often leads to worse suffering.

In conclusion, I believe that legalising euthanasia would be a good thing, and would make perfect sense from a moral, economical and human rights standpoint.

Q25.

I agree with the above statement. I believe that patriotism is a flawed concept, with a number of issues. These are as follows:

Firstly, I would argue that patriotism is subconsciously xenophobic. We are all members of the human race, and are no different to one another. Countries are just arbitrary borders designed to enforce the idea that English are different from Spanish, Italians from Germans etc. This is not healthy, and often leads to a severe clash of cultures. Human beings are human beings, regardless of where on the Earth they reside. Although there is a difference between patriotism and nationalism, patriotism breeds nationalism. By enforcing an unnecessary and unhealthy idea that people of one nation are different from those of another, we generate tension between countries, which leads to a sense of hatred from disenchanted individuals. This results in extremist behaviour, and accelerates global conflicts.

Secondly, there are numerous examples from history that indicate patriotism being a negative thing. Primary amongst these is the world wars. In particular World War 2 was caused by extreme national pride (in Germany). Combined with severe social unrest, this led to an uprising which resulted in the deaths of millions of people.

You could also argue that despite the success of events such as the World Cup, there is still an underlying xenophobia prevalent from the citizens of each nation towards other nations. i.e. the English are rooting against the Italians, or the Germans, or the Spanish. Such events could easily be held without this. Often, it leads to people who aren't patriotic being ostracised or treated as traitors. This is not healthy.

In conclusion, I believe that patriotism is a fundamentally flawed concept, which subconsciously encourages people to foster resentment or animosity towards other, based simply on what country they come from. The country you are born in is ultimately down to chance, so why celebrate this?

A Few Final Words...

You have now reached the end of your IELTS guide and no doubt you feel more prepared to tackle your assessment. We hope you have found this guide an invaluable insight into the questions, and understand the expectations regarding your assessment.

For any type of test, we believe there are a few things to remember in order to better your chances and increase your overall performance.

REMEMBER – THE THREE Ps!

1. Preparation. This may seem relatively obvious, but you will be surprised by how many people fail their assessment because they lacked preparation and knowledge regarding their test. You want to do your utmost to guarantee the best possible chance of succeeding. Be sure to conduct as much preparation prior to your assessment to ensure you are fully aware and 100% prepared to complete the test successfully. Not only will practising guarantee to better your chances of successfully passing, but it will also make you feel at ease by providing you with knowledge and know-how to pass your IELTS academic writing test.

2. Perseverance. You are far more likely to succeed at something if you continuously set out to achieve it. Everybody comes across times whereby they are setback or find obstacles in the way of their goals. The important thing to remember when this happens, is to use those setbacks and obstacles as a way of progressing. It is what you do with your past experiences that helps to determine your success in the future. If you fail at something, consider 'why' you have failed. This will allow you to improve and enhance your performance for next time.

3. Performance. Your performance will determine whether or not you are likely to succeed. Attributes that are often associated with performance are self-belief, motivation and commitment. Self-belief is important for anything you do in life. It allows you to recognise your own abilities and skills and believe that you can do well. Believing that you can do well is half the battle! Being fully motivated and committed is often difficult for some people, but we can assure you that, nothing is gained without hard work and determination. If you want to succeed, you will need to put in that extra time and hard work!

A Few Final Words...

Good luck with your IELTS Academic Writing Test. We would like to wish you the best of luck with all your future endeavours.

The how2become team

The How2Become Team

CHECK OUT OUR OTHER IELTS GUIDE:

FOR MORE INFORMATION ON OUR REVISION GUIDES, PLEASE CHECK OUT THE FOLLOWING:

WWW.HOW2BECOME.COM

Get Access To

FREE

Psychometric Tests

www.PsychometricTestsOnline.co.uk

WANT TO LEARN EVEN MORE REVISION TRICKS?

CHECK OUT OUR OTHER GUIDES:

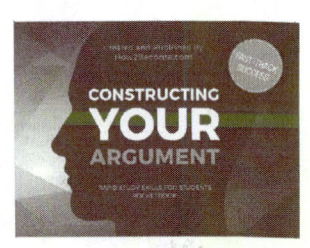

FOR MORE INFORMATION CHECK OUT THE FOLLOWING:

WWW.HOW2BECOME.COM